Praise for *R*
Business

'Growth is one thing. Remarkable growth is even more complex and requires hard work, skill and a plan. This book is your plan.'

Dan Tyre, *Sales Director of HubSpot*

'Today's buyers have changed, and you must evolve your marketing and sales if you want to grow your business. In his book *Remarkable Business Growth*, Richard shares what you need to evolve and how to evolve it in a structured step-by-step methodology that will guarantee you grow in a remarkable way. If you want to grow your B2B business, then you need to read this book.'

Marcus Sheridan, *author of* They Ask, You Answer, *keynote speaker on Digital Sales/Marketing and ranked #1 LinkedIn Voices for Entrepreneurship*

'There are many moving parts in business. However, *Remarkable Business Growth* manages to distil them into a powerful playbook for predictable revenue growth. You will discover the critical role that strategy, processes and systems play in modern business. Read this book, apply it and reap the rewards.'

David Jenyns, *founder of SystemHUB, author of* Systemology

'Richard's book will have you gripped. Richard speaks from experience, having been in business for 30 years and worked with hundreds of small businesses. For many business owners they plateau and the once exciting business becomes a trap. Richard studies the data and provides practical advice. The STEPS methodology that Richard puts forward provides a blueprint of predictability in the unknown waters of entrepreneurship. This arms the small business owner with a compass. This book is a secret weapon, providing clarity and confidence in scaling to seven figures. If you are looking for reassurance, strategy and a surge of new passion to grow your business, then this book will not disappoint.'

Sebastian Bates, *founder of non profit 'Bates Foundation',*
CEO of The Warrior Academy LLC

'Read Richard Mawer's *Remarkable Business Growth* and you'll see your business in a new light and be left with a clear vision of how to take it to the next level.'

Richard Warrilow, *founder of Declaration Ltd*

'I really enjoyed reading *Remarkable Business Growth*. It exceeded my expectations in that Richard has provided a comprehensive roadmap to help businesses grow from being one of the many turning over £350–500k, to that much rarer seven-figure business.'

Austen Hempstead, *owner of Selling is a Skill*

'*Remarkable Business Growth* has all those essential business ideas that we all know we need but never have the time to implement. Richard's book lays it all out in clear, easy to understand terms, so much so that there's really no excuse for not executing them.'

David Allen, *owner of Allen Signs*

'Richard's knowledge and expertise in business growth through inbound marketing and sales is immense. Having so much actionable information on business growth in his book *Remarkable Business Growth* is wonderful, it allows me to identify what needs to be done and then go and apply this knowledge to my business – incredible!'

Gary Davies, *owner of GD Photography*

'I've had the pleasure of reading Richard's new book *Remarkable Business Growth* and can honestly say it is a real page turner! The conversational tone made me feel as though he was in the room with me. Richard's tips, practical advice, and methodology of identifying the process of remarkable growth in simple, clear steps are perfect.'

Tony Smith, *Director of Genius Technology Solutions*

'Through this book, Richard lays out his systematic and essential formula to develop and implement effective strategy for business growth, whilst encouraging the reader to continually seek and thrive for more "remarkable" results.'

Richard Bell, *Director of Neuro Education*

RICHARD MAWER

REMARKABLE BUSINESS GROWTH

Your blueprint for 7 figures and beyond

First published in Great Britain by Practical Inspiration
Publishing, 2023

ISBN   9781788604291   (print)
        9781788604314   (epub)
        9781788604307   (mobi)

Want to bulk-buy copies of this book for your team and
colleagues? We can customise the content and co-brand
Remarkable Business Growth to suit your business's needs.

Please email info@practicalinspiration.com for more details.

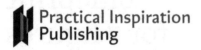

Contents

Contents

Dedication

This book is dedicated to my parents, who showed me the joy and pain of being self-employed, giving me the resilience to battle through the tough times while teaching me to enjoy the small wins along the way. They both demonstrated that life is a journey, not a destination. Thank you to Sandra Mawer (later Dexter) and Gordon Mawer, both gone but never forgotten. No one could ask for better role models.

Foreword by Dan Tyre, Sales Director, HubSpot

Have you ever met a company that didn't want to grow? Rarely do I meet business owners who are content to stay flat year to year. Most motivated business people have the will to grow, the desire to grow, but they lack an understanding of the specific steps required to build the foundation of a seven-figure company. The growth curve remains a mystery.

In the old days (before 2017) businesses could be fairly straightforward. Competition was limited by location and customer need. The pace was steady, and a well-run business could grow at the industry growth rate by executing on the basics. But growing a business in the 21st century is a totally different challenge based on a myriad of unique challenges that all business owners grapple with: hiring and retaining quality employees, technology complexity, product innovation, outmanoeuvring vicious competition, the impact of global events, building a sales and market machine and achieving a sustainable competitive advantage, all while dealing with the ever-changing priorities required to navigate the minefield of the modern business world.

This book explains the transformation from the old world to the modern 'buyer economy', where customers have all the power, expectations are intense, competition comes from every corner of the internet, and business owners have to navigate a new set of rules in order to grow.

Richard Mawer is an expert in the transformation of global business into the online era. He has hundreds of real-life examples of helping companies in many different vertical markets to improve sales, marketing, operations and delivery via an 'inbound' philosophy. He has defined the playbook for hyper-growth businesses that need a good balance between strategy and execution and want to leverage best practices of process and scale. He has then refined the playbook to give you a step-by-step instruction guide to set you up for success.

One of the repeat tenets of his recommendations includes defining the formula for creating repeatable processes that can be documented, studied and improved. Richard also highlights the five stages of business growth from the Set-Up Phase to the Performance Phase and what to do in each and explains how your website is an indispensable tool for creating differentiation and advantage.

This book outlines a thoughtful, intelligent method that effective business leaders can use to their advantage to scale better leveraging processes and technology. The techniques in this book are designed to help leaders keep their sanity as their company stretches to a hyper-growth of 100% annual increases over a period of time – or what Richard describes as 'remarkable growth'.

Over the past decade, there have been hundreds of business books that give business owners the high-level strategy of WHAT to do to scale their business but lack the specific details of HOW to do it. This is not one of those books. My friend and entrepreneur Richard Mawer decided to write a book that would give you a blueprint for a specific scale to get to £1m annual revenue, a significant milestone for any company looking to thrive and then to keep going with remarkable growth.

Having helped to scale five start-ups over the last 42 years (all to over $1m annual revenue, two to over $1bn) and advised thousands of companies on how to scale in the modern era, I completely agree with the format outlined in this book.

Richard eloquently describes the benefits of (1) having a written business growth strategy and trackable forecast; (2) focusing on the most important priorities at each stage; (3) knowing what metrics to measure as your numbers; (4) identify and fixing the gaps; and (5) managing your processes for a predictable outcome.

This methodology can help companies who want to scale fast to start off on the right foot. It can help companies who are flat or trending down to reverse this trend, outlining best practices to make sure they are doing all the right things, at the right time, to turn it around, and it can help growing companies #growbetter.

Growth is one thing. Remarkable growth is even more complex and requires hard work, skill and a plan. This book is your plan.

Dan Tyre, Sales Director of HubSpot
(www.hubspot.com/dantyre) and author of *The Inbound Organisation* (www.dantyre.com/bio).

Introduction

A remarkable B2B business will double its revenue every 12 months.

The surprise is that these businesses are not large corporates or performance businesses with huge budgets to invest in branding, marketing and market domination. They are small and medium-sized lifestyle businesses that have focused their efforts on being remarkable at every touchpoint they have with their prospects, partners, employees and customers.

So why, then, does the average B2B business take five years to double its revenue?

The majority of business owners I meet are frustrated at the lack of growth in their business; they have worked hard over a number of years to grow a small team, developed a good product, service or solution and have a loyal base of customers generating £350–500k of turnover each year, but they are stuck.

When I dig deeper into this, the problems I hear are the same each time: they lack clarity on what is working, what is not working and what they need to do next. They are frustrated at the lack of time they seem to have to work on the high-value work that they know needs doing to move the business forward and are constantly being pulled back into doing the work in the business. They are stressed out by the financial pressure their business is putting on them and their family. Above all, they have lost the passion and fun they had when they started out and they are starting to resent their business; it has become a grind.

The good news is that any business can become remarkable, and I will share a proven formula to get you there, no matter where you are now. But first, a little about me.

I was born into a family of self-employed business owners; neither my mother nor my father were employees or had an employee mentality. One of my father's favourite sayings was 'I don't want someone else to tell me how much I can earn each month', which summed up the positivity that entrepreneurs have in their blood. My dad owned his own garage and ran a small haulage firm of three lorries in Yorkshire. My mother had set up and ran her own secretarial business – a very early example of outsourcing – where she would do typing and administration work for other businesses.

I saw the hard work they put into their businesses and enjoyed the upsides, going abroad on nice holidays through the 1970s, having new cars and a private education. But I also felt the struggles they had at times, the shortage of money, the stress and the eventual breakdown of their marriage, all the result of being self-employed.

I quickly realised that there was little truth in the saying that the harder you work, the more successful you become. Both my parents worked hard their whole lives, but any success was hard earned, and with every up there was always a down waiting around the corner.

I set up my first business in 1993 and, over the past 30 years, have run eight businesses, including two that I took to seven figures. At present, my main business is Ignite Growth Consultancy, where I work exclusively with business-to-business clients to put in place the right strategies, processes and systems required to break through and grow their businesses to £1m turnover and beyond. I am proud to have supported one client through to a £28m exit and another to an £8m acquisition by following the same methodology I will be sharing with you in this book.

One thing is clear: modern business growth is more planned and predictable than it has ever been before. The good news is that anyone can build a remarkable seven-figure business, especially small businesses, which are more agile than their larger counterparts.

In this book I will show you a method that will help you build a remarkable business, from wherever you are today, to seven figures and beyond.

I will explain why it is critical to become remarkable and why so many businesses struggle to achieve this, and I will share my STEPS methodology for business growth, which has been created over the past seven years to help any business grow in a predictable way.

STEPS is a set of proven processes and systems that systematically addresses the three areas preventing most business owners from growing the business they deserve – strategy, process and systems. Every client I speak to who has worked hard to grow organically to a certain point lacks at least one, but in most cases all three, of these things, and these are at the heart of the methodology. I talk more about STEPS in part two of the book.

Finally, I will map out how you can put this into action to build a seven-figure business that will give you more fun, freedom and fulfilment, whilst allowing you to create a legacy for the future.

The truth is that we live in an age where it has never been easier to grow a £1m business, and anyone can do it. With a little focus, some deep work in the right areas and account-ability to the right results, you can do it too.

By the end of this book, you will have a method for building a remarkable seven-figure business. In each chapter I share 'Go be remarkable' tips, and I unpack the principles and processes for building the business that you deserve. You will be able to take these and apply them to your business. At the end of each chapter you will find a summary and an exercise to help you execute this. I know this will be hard work, but it will also be insightful, rewarding and worth it.

Part 1
Building a remarkable seven-figure business

In 30 years of setting up and running businesses, I genuinely believe that there has never been a better time to build a seven-figure business that will give you more fun, freedom and fulfilment.

As I wrote this book, a theme emerged. It is not only growing to £1m that makes growing a B2B business so fun and fulfilling, but also focusing on building a remarkable business that stands out from the competition in the market. A business that people love to do business with and that is deliberately remarkable at every touchpoint it has with customers, clients, partners, employees and prospective customers.

So don't just settle for building a business focused on revenue. Do something special and 'go be remarkable'.

1. Being remarkable matters

Why seven figures is such an important milestone in business

Over the past 30 years of running my own businesses and helping other people to grow theirs, through my digital agency and now my consultancy, it is clear that something magic happens when a business scales to £1m turnover.

I speak with hundreds of business-to-business (B2B) business owners every year, and this figure is a major goal for them; it is as if they feel that this figure will symbolise success. However, when I dig deeper into why they feel like this and I think through the businesses I took to this level, it is not the financial achievement of reaching this milestone that stands out but the journey that comes with it. Yes, having a nice six-figure profit relieves much of the financial pressure you went through during the early years in business, but it is more than the money.

At the heart of it is the fact that you cannot do this on your own; you may be highly skilled and hardworking, but that will only take you so far. In my experience, a high majority of business owners who organically grow their businesses up to the £500k mark do this predominantly by working in their business with a small team around them. The problem is that they then become stuck, no matter how hard they work; they stop growing and this becomes a major frustration, as they are pushing harder and harder for small gains.

It is inevitable that you will reach a point where you do not have the right strategy, processes and systems in place to keep growing. You will struggle to find the clarity on what to do next, you will struggle to attract the right talent into your business to support your growth and, most importantly, you will reach a point where you will not have the time to work on the high-value strategic work that will help you break out of this situation, as you will constantly be dragged back into the business to deliver for clients.

Over the next few chapters I will cover how to put in place the right strategy, processes and systems to change this dynamic, but first let's take a look at why the lack of one or all of these is so critical to your business growth.

Strategy – The lack of a structured plan or strategy is the reason why you will struggle to find clarity on what is working and not working with your business growth and, more importantly, what to do about it. No strategy means you have no clear plan on what is being executed on a daily basis and no clearly defined milestones and goals to hit.

Processes – The lack of clearly defined processes and procedures for how you do what you do is a major reason why you will struggle to find consistency in delivery. More importantly, this is the fundamental reason that you, as the business owner, are still doing the low-value work in your business rather than releasing yourself to focus on the high-value strategic work. Great processes are the engine that drives predictable growth in every business.

Systems – The lack of a modern connected system of technology, tools and software pulling all of this together in your business will severely hamper your growth. No matter how hard you work, you must embrace technology and leverage it to scale predictably. The majority of businesses

I speak to have built a system organically, adding multiple pieces of software in a random manner, usually driven by a particular person or function rather than with the overall business growth goals in mind.

As you can see, hard work can get you so far when growing your business, but eventually you will reach a point where the lack of strategy, processes and systems is going to work against you and result in that frustration we have all felt, where we are working harder and harder in our business but seeing no progress. The good news is you are not on your own.

A good example is Sebastian Bates, a friend and mentor of mine who runs a business called The Warrior Academy.[1] In 2010, Seb had been training out in Thailand as a Thai boxer and competing in competitions before he decided to return to the UK. On his return, he set up a company called Warrior Thai Boxing and later The Warrior Academy in 2011. He ran the business over the next six years, figuring it out as he went.

Seb admits that, through hard work, he slowly grew revenue to £234k, but it was always a struggle until he sat down and planned out a more structured strategy for growth in 2018 and started processing out what he did in the business with a view to expanding it, not just in the UK but also globally.

This strategy and process work resulted in a strategic move to Dubai. Seb realised that there was a real opportunity to use martial arts for character development in the UAE, so he moved to Dubai in January 2019 and placed some Facebook ads. One of the people to respond was a PA to the royal family of Dubai, who asked him to train the children of the royal family. The effect of this move was to see an 85%

---

[1] www.warrioracademy.co.uk

increase in revenue to £433k. In 2019 he launched his global anti-bullying initiative 'Not A Victim' and continued to grow, even through 2020 and the COVID pandemic. By 2021 he had grown revenue to £1.25m. As he freely admits, all of this was down to putting in place strategy, processes and systems in 2018 to drive the breakthrough.

The five phases of business growth

When I say you are not on your own, I mean it. As Seb's story demonstrates, every business goes through five very predictable phases of growth. I can guarantee that you have been through or are currently going through one of these as you read this book. Each phase presents unique challenges and opportunities to break through to the next level, and each business owner has their own personal goal they would like to reach.

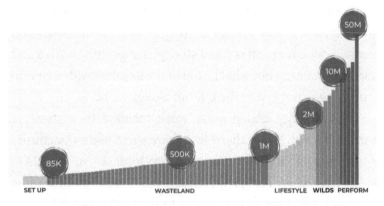

Many entrepreneurs love the energy of the set-up and start-up phase. The majority are happy building to a nice seven-figure lifestyle business that gives good six-figure profits and allows them to live their life completely, whilst some want to build a larger performance business with an eight-figure turnover and seven-figure profits. Let's look at each individually.

The Set-Up Phase – The initial stage of 'set up' is when you start your business, full of excitement and optimism. The first 6–12 months are great fun. You are focusing on proving your concept and developing your offering, and you have plenty of energy for the road ahead. It is just you and maybe one other co-founder. You have the time to do things right, no money worries and only a few clients to take care of. You are loving life and working hard to reach the £85k VAT threshold, which is when you start to transition from being a start-up into organic growth.

The Wasteland Phase – This is the organic growth phase that every business moves into once it has survived the initial 12 months. Now the hard work of building a team, taking on more clients and increasing revenue starts to hit home. The owner and co-founder split responsibilities based on their personalities and skill sets, with one usually being more numbers and admin focused and the other being the creative force that drives the business forward, develops the product, service or solution and delivers to clients. The team slowly grows to five or six people, and the financial pressures of wages, larger premises and operational delivery start to grow.

The Lifestyle Phase – Something magical happens as the business grows through the wasteland to become a true lifestyle business at around £1m turnover. You are producing nice six-figure profits so the financial pressure starts to ease, and your team has grown to 10 or 12 people, with a focus on operational delivery for clients, a marketing and sales function and financial support. You now have more time to focus on the high-value strategic work rather than lower value administration and operational delivery tasks. The fun returns to the business and you find that a very dynamic, focused environment develops as you push towards £2m turnover, with a small highly skilled team around you.

As the business owner, you now have a tough decision to make: do you stay here as a lifestyle business or grow again to become a larger performance business.

The Wilds Phase – This is a critical time for both the business and you as the owner. There is the lure of growing towards eight figures and seven-figure profits, but to get there you will have to restructure and go through more growing pains. The dynamic of what you built in the life-style phase will totally change in your business. Everything is about scale and growing a high-performance team, initially scaling up to 30 people and then on towards 50 or 60 employees. The struggles you went through in the wasteland phase now appear small, as you have to deal with this transition, more compliance issues, the development of a senior management team and board, and large marketing and sales functions capable of producing the volume of leads and revenue required to grow to £10m+ revenue. Again, you will have less and less time, as you will be constantly firefighting and managing the growth of the organisation.

The Performance Phase – Battle through the wilds and you arrive here. You own a performance business with a board of directors, a high-performing team and growing revenues. You start to attract interest from serious investors, larger businesses see you as an acquisition target and you can think about exiting for a life-changing amount of money. The reality is that less than 5% of businesses successfully make it to this level, and it is rare for the original owners and team to still be involved when they do.

Every owner will have their own drivers and goals: some will be happy at £350k turnover and a small team, while others will always want to keep pushing forward and grow their business. Develop the self-awareness to know what will make you happy and be prepared to work hard to get there.

Unfortunately, the wasteland phase of growth is where I meet 75% of business owners I talk to and work with. They are stuck at £350–500k turnover, overwhelmed, stressed and frustrated. The good news is that it doesn't have to be that way, so let's start to look at how you can build the business you deserve.

The world has changed, has your business?

The world has changed so much for businesses over the past 30 years when I think back to my first business in 1993 and how technology has impacted every area of business life since then. The internet has grown from something academics set up and used to something that society cannot live without. I remember Microsoft launching Windows 95 and how that suddenly gave us all the ability to easily access the internet and send emails at scale. Then there was the growth of the search engines and the dominance of Google, followed by the explosion of social media from the early days of Web 2.0 and Myspace through to the current dominance of Facebook, Twitter, YouTube, TikTok, Instagram, Snapchat and LinkedIn. It has been a sea-change for society, and the impact on business has been profound. The way we consume content, the time we spend on social media and the way we do our own research before ever reaching out to a business has caused the biggest shift, which is in how we all make buying decisions.

It has forced businesses through a period of digital transformation, resulting in a transition in the way they use technology in every area of their organisation, driven by the changing buying habits and decision-making processes of customers. The way a prospective customer researches and buys a service, product or solution has changed forever, especially in the business-to-business space.

The simple fact is that if you don't align how you market and sell your services with how the modern buyer researches and buys, you will never grow your business and will be constantly fighting the changing world rather than working with it. The old ways of broadcasting and interrupting people's attention are expensive and ineffective – it damages your reputation – so you are better off offering valuable insights to attract people by sharing what you know, answering their questions and addressing their challenges, as this will be the only way to cut through the noise to connect and engage with them.

Stop being a megaphone broadcasting and interrupting people and become the magnet that attracts them and pulls them in with engaging content.

As if the seismic shift in decision-making was not enough, a further impact has been in globalisation – the fact that you are no longer competing on a local or even a national level for the attention of your audience. In many sectors you face global markets and offerings from organisations across the world.

Your customers are now demanding a personal service and personalisation of their user experience, from your website through your sales process, operational delivery and service/support. The personalisation of what you do is no longer simply a 'nice to have' – it is expected by your customers.

Finally, probably the most important factor to rise from these changes is the sheer volume of noise that we are bombarded with on a daily basis from people trying to get our attention. How many marketing and sales messages do you receive in your email or on social media when you are browsing, let alone through traditional media such as television, radio and print?

The remarkable principle of differentiation

Yet, through all of this change, remarkable businesses of all sizes have emerged that are thriving, businesses that are resilient to the state of the economy, have successfully embraced digital technology and continue to double their revenue year on year.

Stop for a moment and imagine what your life would be like if you could grow your business by doubling your revenue every 12 months. What difference would that make not only to your work life but, more importantly, to your personal life and the type of life you could live?

So how do you build a remarkable business and differentiate yourself to get the attention of your audience, giving you a competitive advantage to dominate your market? You need to build a business that people remark about and comment on and that stays front of mind, a remarkable business that connects with people emotionally and logically.

> **Definition of remarkable:** The Oxford Dictionary definition of remarkable is 'something that is worthy of attention; striking'.

At the end of this chapter I will ask you to take the time to audit each of the touchpoints you have with people and assess whether they are remarkable, average or poor.

Take the time now to think through these 15 touchpoints. This is not an exhaustive list but will start your thought process.

- Website
- Landing pages
- Social media
- Brochures
- Trade show stand (if you have one)
- Banners
- Webinars/podcasts
- Blog content
- Conversion content – PDF/white papers/reports/checklists
- Videos
- Graphics
- Emails
- Sales process
- Operational delivery
- Customer service/support

How remarkable is your business in each of these areas? Imagine if every one of these was remarkable and left a prospect, client, partner or even your employees saying 'wow'. Do you think this would differentiate you in your market?

But it is not just about differentiation. When you build a remarkable business, you build a business that not only has a real competitive advantage in your market but is also resilient to changes in environment and the economy.

I hear so many experts waxing lyrical about 'business resilience' and theorising on how to build this into your business so you can manage skills gaps, an ageing workforce, the lack of talent, the impact of a fluctuating economy and any number of 'crisis management' scenarios, such as Brexit, pandemics, energy costs, rising transportation costs and global events.

But when you have a remarkable business that is doubling revenue every year, none of this matters. You attract the right talent that wants to work for you and have the resources to ride out any crisis, resources that are not subject to fluctuations in the economy. Remarkable resilience is built in.

Be remarkable in your drive to seven figures

I hope you are starting to realise that this is not all about being a large corporate. The businesses that benefit the most from the remarkable mindset are the micro and small businesses that have a real intent to grow. They are more agile and can create more of an impact in their sectors by focusing on making each touchpoint remarkable.

It is no longer good enough for you to simply go through the motions of creating a strategy, developing processes and pulling together a system of software, tools and technology. You must focus on continually innovating, disrupting and evolving every touchpoint you have with your prospects, employees, partners and customers to become 'remarkable'.

Summary

If you are like the majority of the five million business owners across the UK, and particularly those that I speak to on a daily basis, you probably set up your business for one of four reasons. I call this the 'Founder Principle', as why you set up your business can determine how easy you find it to grow it.

You probably set your business up because:

- you identified a gap in the market
- you realised that there was a better way to do something
- you developed a set of skills working for someone else and decided you would rather do it for yourself
- you got the opportunity to take over an existing business, normally a family business that you worked in and took over when someone retired.

You will have grown a small team and loyal customer base who love you and what you do, slowly increasing revenue year on year, with monthly variations, but getting to around £350–£500k turnover after five years and then stopping or, even worse, going backwards.

I guarantee that this will be due to the lack of strategy, processes and systems to grow to seven figures and beyond.

Alongside this I am going to recommend that you focus on becoming remarkable in every area of your business, but predominantly in those key touchpoints you have with your prospects, customers and partners on a daily basis.

Over the course of this book, we are going to explore the what and the how of becoming a remarkable seven-figure business, and I will share with you a proven methodology to achieve the business you deserve, a business that will give you more fun, freedom and fulfilment than ever before.

Exercise #1 – Your remarkable audit

How remarkable is your business at present?

Go to www.goberemarkable.com/resources and download the Remarkable Audit worksheet. Take the time to complete the exercise by working through each of the 15 touchpoints and marking yourself on how remarkable you are at present.

Do not move onto Chapter 2 until you have completed this activity on your business.

2. The strategy principle

Strategy drives your tactics

The big idea behind planning a strategy is that in every remarkable business it's the strategy that drives the tactical execution on a daily basis and not the tactics that drive the strategy.

When I talk about planning out a detailed strategy, I do not mean a business plan, a marketing plan or a sales plan. I mean an effective growth strategy that will predictably get you from where you are now to your revenue goals.

Strategy will tell you *what*, but the power is in the *how*

One of my favourite stories of strategy vs tactics is Clayton Christensen's account of meeting Andy Grove, one of the original founders of Intel, as a consultant to help with the launch of the Celeron processor. Clayton was the Professor of Business Administration at the Harvard Business School and author of *The Innovator's Dilemma*, in which he demonstrated his expertise in disruptive innovation. He had been brought in by Intel as a consultant to discuss tactics to counter the impact of cut-price processors hitting the market, such as AMD's chips, that were eating into their market share. In one of the breaks during a number of long theoretical discussions, Grove asked, 'How do I do this?', to which Christensen launched into a discussion of business strategy. Grove cut him off, saying: 'You are such a naïve academic. I asked you how to do it and you told me what I should do. I know what I need to do. I just don't know how to do it.'[2]

In this chapter I am going to focus on the 'what' you need in your growth strategy, then, as you start looking at the 'how' and creating your strategy in Chapter 5, following the STEPS methodology, it will all start to come together for you.

Do you use satnav or a map?

When talking with clients, I always discuss the analogy of going on a long car journey, especially to somewhere new that you have not visited before. You plan out many of the details for your trip; you don't just jump in your car and hope to get there.

You plan a route, prepare the vehicle for the trip, fill up with fuel, put the destination in your satnav or, if you are old school, get the map book out (I still love to do that), then head for your destination.

Mapping out a structured growth strategy will give you clarity on where you are going (your revenue goals), how you are going to get there (the tactics to focus on) and total clarity for you and your team on whether you are on or off track.

Yet I still meet so many business owners who are 'winging it' or on autopilot, just driving every day without a clearly defined destination. Obviously, this is not how you are going to build a remarkable seven-figure business, so let's change the approach.

---

[2] C. Christensen, 'Foreword to the First Edition', in C. McChesney, S. Covey, J. Huling, B. Walker, and S. Thele, *The 4 Disciplines of Execution: Achieving your Wildly Important Goals*, pp. xv–xviii (2021).

Adopting a strategy-first approach

In my agency, Digital Media Edge, our focus with clients was always on strategy first rather than simply offering a tactical solution to their growth challenges, which is what the majority of other agencies do. We felt this was so critical to success that it would often determine whether we worked with a client or not. Our starting point was in understanding their specific goals, challenges, gaps, opportunities and timescales. We knew that all of these were critical to planning out an effective growth strategy.

The feedback we got over the seven years of running the business was that it was very unusual for a digital agency to focus on strategy, as opposed to trying to sell solutions that we had the skill set for in-house – i.e., website development, inbound marketing services, search engine optimisation, content creation, video creation or PR services.

The differentiation for us was clear: it set us apart from other agencies who focused heavily on the skills they had and then selling these skills to as many clients as they could find.

At DME we positioned ourselves intentionally as a growth agency; our focus was on helping our B2B clients to grow better, and to achieve this we had to understand each client's intent to grow and how we could support this, then identify the tactics to focus on in order to deliver the growth. We understood that a detailed growth strategy would drive remarkable tactical execution.

Remember that clarity comes from looking at your business through a strategic lens, and whenever you are lacking clarity, it is usually because you are not thinking strategically but tactically.

Remarkable businesses are aligned internally and externally. A detailed measurable strategy also ensures alignment in your business. If you communicate your strategy and the metrics that are being measured regularly with your team, then they will align around the achievement of these goals and understand their role in the overall strategy.

Finally, developing a strategy will take you deep into understanding your buyer's world, so your strategy will also align how you market and sell with how that buyer researches and buys. You will therefore position yourself more effectively in the market and buyers will understand who you help, how you help them and why you do it better than anyone else.

Start by getting specific with your revenue growth goals

Let's be honest. Before you start to plan a growth strategy to map out where you want to go, you need to know where you are now and a specific destination that you want to get to.

My goal in this book is to put in place all the elements you need to build a remarkable business that will take you to seven figures and beyond. But for now, let's put down £1m as our specific revenue goal.

Now we are going to reverse engineer your revenue funnel.

Where are you now? Take a look at your past three years' turnover. Is it static or fluctuating?

Work out where you are now for revenue. We have our starting point.

Now break it down to a timescale and be realistic, as you need to be able to deliver on this too.

For example, it is unrealistic to set a revenue goal of £1m in the next 12 months if you are currently at £350k and have been growing by £25k a year for the past five years, but it may be perfectly realistic if you are already at £700k per year.

Set yourself a 12-month goal. Again, be specific about what net new revenue you need to generate, assuming your current revenue remains the same. So you would give yourself a goal of, say, 'We will hit £600k turnover by 31 December and this will include generating £100k of net new revenue.'

Now get some other key revenue metrics together to help you plan out your growth strategy.

What is your average order value (AOV)? Take your past 100 orders placed and average this out to get a figure. Do not split it by product or service cost at this stage; you just need the average figure from the last 100 transactions. Remember the importance of this is that you can focus part of your sales strategy on increasing your AOV figure and identify tactics to do this.

How many orders do you need to hit your revenue goal? This is quite a straightforward calculation at this point, but it gives you a solid KPI to measure progress against. Are you on or off track to hit this? You can also break this down seasonally or monthly, depending on the sales cycle in your business.

What is your current sales conversion rate from lead to order percentage? Avoid guesswork here. If you are not measuring all your lead sources and cannot get an accurate figure for average conversion percentage, then make this a priority of your strategy and start recording as soon as possible. A rule of thumb is an average B2B lead conversion rate of 1 in 5 or 20%. I hope you can see why this figure is so important, as, by simply optimising this metric to 1 in 4 or 25%, you significantly increase revenue without generating any additional leads or traffic.

How many leads are you currently generating per month? At this stage you just need a total monthly figure. I recommend that you audit all of your lead sources here and measure each of them for effectiveness, too. How are you measuring what a lead is? Do you have a lead matrix in place that identifies what a good lead is? What is the total number of leads you are generating per month?

What is your current website conversion rate (visitors to leads)? As a rule of thumb, you should be aiming to achieve a 2% conversion rate of website visitors into leads in your CRM. For example, if you are seeing 600 visitors to your website on a monthly basis, you should be generating 12 active leads per month. When I start working with clients, their visitors-to-leads conversion rate tends to be around 0.01%, as they have not optimised their website for conversions. Where are you now?

How many website visitors do you currently have each month? If you have Google Analytics set up, then this is a straightforward report to run. I would run a report for annual traffic to your website and then divide by twelve for a monthly average. Check for any obvious monthly trends if you have any kind of seasonal element to your business, but the goal is to keep this as flat and consistent as possible.

These core metrics are the foundation for your business growth and will form your KPIs and your lag and lead metrics going forward, so take your time going through Exercise #2 at the end of this chapter.

The direct impact of strategy on revenue

When I set up my agency Digital Media Edge, we grew organically, with revenue of £180k in 2015 and then £220k by the end of 2016.

We always seemed to be chasing work and taking every job we could. As we only had a small team, I personally was doing a lot of the work, which was stopping me from focusing on the high-value work of planning a strategy for the business.

In January 2018, I realised that my focus had to switch from tactical implementation to strategic planning. I mapped out a far more detailed strategy for growth, including how we were going to grow the team from two to six, the finance we would need in place to do so and the systems we would need.

We also joined HubSpot as an agency partner to give us the tools to grow and scale. The result was an increase in revenue from £283k in 2017 to £575k in 2018 and a platform to kick on towards seven figures.

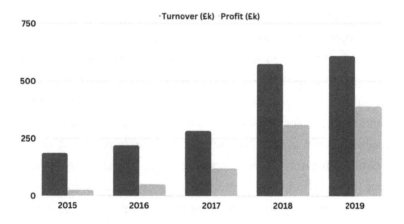

As a direct result of this strategic work, we also attracted investment from a client who we had been working with for 18 months through to his exit of £28m. He invested a significant sum for 20% of the business.

None of this would have been possible without a structured plan and strategy in place that provided clarity to align the team and make decisions.

Your strategy within a strategy

Once you have an overall strategic goal and objective, with some key metrics and milestones in place, the other elements within your strategy will start to fall into place, as they feed into the overall revenue goal achievement.

The following six key elements will give you the basis of a strategy:

Targeting Strategy – Who are you targeting specifically, what sector or industry, then what people within the companies within that sector? This will become your Target Account List (more about that in Chapter 5). You must go narrow and deep, not broad and wide. Map out your Ideal Customer Profile and Primary Buyer Personas.

Website Design and Development Strategy – Use the homepage to position exactly who you help, how you help them and why you do it better than anyone else. Create a remarkable user experience on every device, including mobile. Build out a community and resources that solve people's questions, challenges and the mistakes they are making and help them make the right decision for them. Focus everything on converting visitors into engaged users and leads in your CRM. Aim for a 2% visitor-to-customer conversion rate, then improve on this.

Sales Plan and Strategy – Your sales plan will come before your marketing plan, as this will help you identify the types of campaigns and support, including the number of leads you need to generate from your marketing efforts. Focus on customer acquisition, including a step-by-step sales process and pipeline development with metrics for activity such as calls, emails, meetings, presentations and revenue generated.

Marketing Plan and Strategy – Focused on lead generation processes, including content strategy, social media strategy, conversion offers, landing pages, forms, calls to action and metrics for engagement and leads. As discussed above, once you know your revenue goals and your sales goals, you must sit down and plan out what your marketing campaigns will look like, what content and campaign assets need developing to support those campaigns and what metrics you will measure to track the effectiveness of your marketing.

Operational Delivery Strategy – How are you going to make the delivery of your core services remarkable and delight your customers? You must plan this out, including what processes you need to develop to make remarkable delivery of your services happen every time.

Service and Support Strategy – How will you continue to delight your customers? Do you have in place a way to survey customers? Do you have a process to ask for reviews from happy customers? How do you generate testimonials and case studies? Do you routinely ask for referrals? Are you listening and acting on your customer's feedback to evolve your offering and develop new offerings?

As you can see, to develop a remarkable growth strategy you need to bring together multiple elements of your business and plan a mini-strategy for each that feeds into the overall revenue growth goals of your business. I cover exactly how to achieve this in Chapter 5 and Chapter 6.

Identifying your challenges, gaps and opportunities

The final part of planning out the 'what' of your growth strategy is to be realistic and take a deep dive into your challenges, gaps and opportunities for growth.

Challenges

To identify your challenges to growth, focus on the top-of-the-funnel challenges you face. Take a look at your website traffic levels, website user experience, website conversion rates and the number of leads you are generating on a monthly basis. Are you getting in front of the eyeballs of your Primary Buyer Persona and getting their attention?

Gaps

Next, take a look at anything you are short of – your gaps. These will usually be in the resources, knowledge or technology you need in place to enable growth. Do you need to employ a new person or bring in expertise from external sources to plug these gaps and ensure that these do not block your strategy for growth?

Opportunities – Low hanging fruit and early quick wins

Finally, identify your opportunities for growth in revenue. We are looking here for the low hanging fruit and the quick wins that your strategy can enable in order to give it momentum. Again, my advice here is to look at two key areas:

Conversion optimisation – Optimising website conversions and sales conversions will produce more leads but with the same level of traffic. The majority of businesses I meet say they need more traffic and leads, but when I start to dig into the levels they already have, I find they have more than enough. The problem is not lead generation but conversion. There is little point in pouring more traffic into a leaky bucket.

Existing customers – How effective are you at engaging with your existing base of customers? The biggest opportunity I find for most businesses is in their existing customers. When we run re-engagement campaigns to their customer lists, it always generates three or four new orders. Client engagement is a key part of being remarkable, as we will discuss with the process principle and in Chapter 8 on promoters.

You are now ready to start creating and planning out a detailed, measurable growth strategy that will propel you toward seven figures, smash through any challenges you have, address the gaps in your business and maximise your opportunities for growth. But more of that in Chapter 5, when we will use the STEPS method to create your strategy.

Summary

The big idea is to put in place an effective strategy that will drive your daily execution. A strategy that will:

- give you total clarity on what you are doing every day and why
- provide key metrics, allowing you to measure progress and whether you are on or off track

- align everyone in your business around your revenue goals
- give clarity to your position in the market and in the eyes of your buyers so it is clear who you help, how you help them and why you do it better than anyone else in your sector.

Spend at least three months putting together a measurable growth strategy that you can communicate across your business.

Once you have done this, you will have a remarkable strategy in place and ready to execute.

Go be remarkable: Once you complete your growth strategy, set up a Strategy Launch Day to align everyone in the business around your new strategy. In my experience, these are one of the most powerful ways to get full buy-in from your team and kick-start a strategy.

Exercise #2 – Know your numbers

Identify what your annual revenue goals are and the milestones you need to hit to get there.

Go to www.goberemarkable.com/resources and download the Know Your Numbers worksheet. Take the time to complete the exercise and calculate each of the 10 top-level metrics you will measure to show you are on or off track.

3. The process principle

Designing your engine for predictable business growth

Great processes are the machine at the heart of a remarkable business and growth; they ensure that your growth is both predictable and measurable. The direct impact that process and procedure have on every area of your business growth cannot be overstated; they are without doubt the most valuable assets in any business and, if you ever come to an exit or acquisition, they will have a direct impact on the value of your business.

However, the biggest impact they will have on you as a business owner is to release you from doing the low-value work in your business on a daily basis, freeing up your time and allowing you to focus on the high-value strategic work that needs doing to keep you moving towards your goals.

So if you are still being forced to work in your business on a daily basis to do administrative tasks or deliver your product, service or solution to clients, leaving yourself stressed and with little time to do anything else, then this is the answer. You will see that the exercise at the end of this chapter is focused on you freeing up your time. When we get to the STEPS methodology for execution in Chapters 5–10, you will see that three of the five elements revolve around creating remarkable processes in your business and the key areas to develop processes for.

I have many clients who tell me that focusing on process and procedures was the game changer in their business growth. Process is nothing new and we have had standard operating procedures for many years in business, but one of the impacts of technology and software doing some of the heavy lifting for us is that people do not put the work into manually setting up a process first, then finding software to automate it.

The main reasons to develop processes and procedures are:

- to document your unique way of doing something
- to build resilience into your business and ensure you have more options
- to measure each step of how you do things
- to optimise your processes to evolve and improve every area of your business.

In every remarkable business there is a constant evolution driven by executing, measuring and optimising to improve everything they do. If you can introduce this approach into your business, then you will be adding a valuable part of your culture, too, and the 'this is how we do it here' mentality that will be used to attract new talent to your business.

As Daniel Priestley discusses in his book *24 Assets*, the value of systems assets and how processes and procedures make your business repeatable and predictable to run is critical. He talks about operating procedures, manuals, scripts, slide decks, checklists and software that can help to process out what you do.[3]

If you ever come to the point of exiting your business, the value in these processes is tangible, as any purchaser will

---

[3] D. Priestley, *24 Assets* (2017).

want to see that the business will be able to run without you. Whether or not you are going to sell, I believe that this has to be a key driver in the way in which you develop the processes that underpin your business.

Five critical areas to process in your business

As I discussed above, the priority for you is to first process out what you do and especially focus on identifying the low value work that is taking up your time each day.

Once you have done this, and the exercise at the end of the chapter will help, I recommend five areas for you and your team to start working on:

1. **Marketing Processes** – You must document how your lead generation works. I recommend adopting a campaign approach, where you split all your lead sources up and create a campaign for each, then put in place step-by-step procedures for running each campaign, including listing out the assets you need to create and run the campaign. I cover this in detail in Chapters 6 and 7 when I talk about traffic and engagement. The key here is to make your lead generation scalable and predictable so you can increase or decrease it as required. Most businesses never get to this stage and it is because they have not processed it out.

2. **Sales Processes** – After processing your lead generation, you must do the same for your customer acquisition process, as these two form the 'revenue machine' of the business. You will now have a predictable flow of leads into the business. Next is to develop

a step-by-step process that every lead goes through. The process should include the four steps of inbound sales – namely identify, connect, explore and advise. I cover this in detail in Chapter 7.

3.   **Operational Delivery Processes** – How you do what you do is one of the most valuable processes you have in your business, especially as far as user experience and customer delight is concerned. Make sure that you process your operational delivery out. This will help you to constantly improve delivery but will also be one of the assets that a potential buyer would look at to ensure that the performance of the business is consistent and would not suffer were you to exit. I always feel that this also protects your standards and removes the need for you to do the work, as you know that the rest of your team are doing it to the standard you set originally.

4.   **Service and Support Processes** – Your client engagement post-sale is what will set you apart from your competition. A remarkable post-sale experience for customers will continue to delight them, encouraging them to become promoters of your business, make repeat purchases, leave you testimonials, reviews and case studies and give you feedback on how you can improve your service even further by completing your surveys. Finally, a process for driving referrals from happy customers is probably one of the easiest ways to generate good quality leads and increase future revenue for your business.

5.   **Administration Processes** – Finally, focus on the administrative processes and procedures that you follow in your business, especially legal, financial

and recruitment. Your business should run like a machine and things should not happen by chance. You need processes in place for new employees to learn how you like things done and to set the standards and culture in your business. So if you are one of those creative entrepreneurs that hates 'boring' paperwork, you must get someone in who loves it and work with them to create processes for the running of your business. Think about cyber security, data governance and data compliance, as the penalties and other ramifications for getting this wrong can be high.

I hope this helps you appreciate the importance of getting your procedures and processes right in these five areas of the business, as they are critical to developing a remarkable business that can grow predictably. Having them in place also allows you to accurately measure their effectiveness and improve them; these small incremental improvements of your processes will lead to massive gains overall.

The power of process in action

A great example of the power of processes is provided by a client I worked with, The Bluecastle Group, who are an energy and renewables business based in Lincolnshire.

When I started working with them, they were a very traditional business with no digital approach to speak of; they were going through a major transition in how they did business.

The management team and CEO were buying out the original owners, it was 2020 and we were in the middle of the COVID pandemic, and the business had lost a few key people over the year and were putting in place a new sales team and system.

They had developed a new service – a revolutionary new approach to recycling vinyl, particularly the vinyl wrap and pop-up banners that were popular with printers but could not be broken down or recycled. Bluecastle had developed a system that could break vinyl down into individual strands and allow it to be re-used.

The new sales team lacked a structured marketing or sales process and was struggling to generate and convert leads into revenue.

We worked on a strategy and focused on putting in place an account-based marketing campaign process to generate leads by connecting and engaging with the main vinyl producers such as Soyang in Manchester and partnering with them to email the individual printers that they supplied direct. We also set up re-marketing campaigns aimed at the print industry across LinkedIn.

I created a four-step sales process and pipeline to send each lead through, with a metric at each point to measure conversion from one stage to another. On the back of this sales process we created a simple LAPS weekly reporting cadence, where each sales team member reported back on Leads, Appointments, Presentations and Sales (I cover more about the power of LAPS in Chapter 5 and Chapter 10). Finally, we systemised all of this by onboarding the team to HubSpot's CRM, marketing, sales software and tools.

In just over eight weeks, we generated 12 new leads and £21k of revenue, and this same campaign and sales process has continued to work and has now generated the business

£485k net new revenue, as an increasing level of new and repeat sales were generated. I hope you can see the power of a repeatable process.

Seven steps to setting up remarkable processes

When it comes to setting up your procedures and processes, your focus has to be on achieving a standard of consistent delivery and outcomes: this will increase productivity and efficiency. Remember that processes are one of the most valuable assets you have in your business.

In simple terms, a process is little more than a series of steps that someone must take to produce a set outcome, but when doing it for your business there are some rules to follow to make them effective:

1. Document your core business functions. This is vital for removing you from the day-to-day operations of your business.
2. Identify the tools and resources that will be required to complete the process.
3. Produce a checklist for each function as a 'how to' document. My advice here is to first video yourself doing the process, then you can include this video alongside a scripted version of your procedure.
4. Capture your team members' knowledge and add this to the procedure too as part of optimising the process. As I discussed above, everyone in your team will have different skills that they can bring to the process and this knowledge is invaluable.

5. Test the process by doing a few dummy runs. Does it flow? Does it achieve the outcome required by the standard set?

6. Measure, review and revise. Remember that just documenting is not enough; each process needs to be constantly monitored and reviewed regularly to ensure it is still producing. When I am working on processes with clients, I ask them to think: 'Is there a better way to achieve this outcome?'

7. Store centrally and ensure that they are easy to access and update as your procedures evolve. We used Dropbox and Google Drive initially before moving to a cloud-based system that can be accessed by all.

Go be remarkable: Check out SystemHUB,[4] developed by a good friend of mine, David Jenyns, from Melbourne, Australia. Dave is the author of *Systemology*[5] and he has become a global expert on helping businesses to use processes, procedures and systems to create time, reduce errors and scale profits. He originally ran an agency called Melbourne SEO and developed SystemHUB as a way of tracking all his procedures and processes. The cloud-based system allows you to centrally store all your procedures and has the added benefit of allowing you to set update and review dates for each, ensuring that they are always up to date. Dave eventually sold Melbourne SEO in 2019, and the person who bought the business said their two reasons for buying it were 'financial perfor-

---

[4] www.systemHUB.com
[5] www.systemology.com/book

mance and the systems and procedures'. These showed that it was not an owner-operated business or dependant on Dave being involved; it was a machine that was just working. The business sold far quicker and for far more than it would have done without the processes in place.

If you work hard to get these seven steps in place, not only will you produce a set of remarkable operating procedures for every element of your business, but, most importantly, you will also have removed yourself from the day-to-day running of your business, and that is a huge win, as you will now be able to focus your time and energy on high-value strategic development and execution.

Summary – Build your process engine one piece at a time

The process principle is critical to building a remarkable business that will predictably grow towards seven figures and beyond. I will go so far as to say that, without great processes, you will struggle to build the business you deserve.

Like the majority of business owners, I took a long time to realise the importance of processes and procedures, and as I look back at the businesses I ran that did not break through and the revenue flatlined, the reason can be traced back to this simple principle.

It is also a fundamental reason for the lack of clarity and time that the majority of business owners have in their business. Just because you *can* do something, it certainly does not mean you *should*. But it is hard to let go, and the usual reasons I hear are 'But they won't do it as well as me' or 'It is just quicker if I do it'. The lesson I learned was when I employed a marketer to the DME team. She was highly skilled in paid advertising on Google Ads and LinkedIn but needed to be mentored and trained in more traditional inbound and account-based marketing. I discussed this with my operations manager and agreed to document everything I did with a client in each area, then train the new marketer in the way I currently did it and ask her to improve it.

The result was that she took everything I had documented and, as this was her sole focus in a day, she improved it and continued to improve it. I know she did everything 50% better than I ever would have. The processes enabled her to do this and allowed her to bring her existing knowledge into the mix too.

So my message here is to take the time to get this right. Document everything you do and identify what is high value and what is low value, then make sure you build out a 'how to' procedure for each task and delegate everything you can to your team.

Exercise #3 – Free your time and your growth will follow

Go to www.goberemarkable.com/resources and download the Time Planner worksheet.

The focus of this exercise is to record everything you do in a day between 8am and 6pm for the next 14 days. On the Time Planner you can record segments of 30 minutes, there is a column for what type of task you are doing – either marketing, sales, operational, service or administration –

and, finally, there is a column for identifying the priority of the task – 1 is high-value, 2 is mid-value and 3 is low-value.

The goal is to map out a process for all the low-value work you are doing, then delegate it to someone else in your team. Then move to the mid-value tasks and, again, map out a process and identify someone else who can do these tasks. You can now focus on only high-value work in the business, unless you are required to do a mid-value delivery task.

As simple as this sounds, the commitment and discipline required to complete this exercise over two weeks, plus the insights it will give you into where your time is being spent and how much low-value work you are doing in your business, will be an eye opener and make an incredible difference to the time you have available on a daily basis.

So don't procrastinate; commit to doing this now before moving on to the next chapter. Or if you don't want to wait two weeks, then get started now.

4. The systems principle

Remarkable businesses systemise before they optimise

Your priority is to build a connected system of technology, tools and software that is easy to use, acts as your single source of truth and measures everything to allow data-driven decisions to be made on what is working and what is not.

Great systems are the competitive advantage that remarkable businesses have over their competition, no matter what size they are.

I can guarantee that if you lack clarity in your business, then it will be either due to the lack of a strategy being executed on a daily basis or the use of a fragmented, unconnected system that makes it impossible for you to gain a clear picture of the direction in which you are actually taking the business. The data and metrics that keep you informed of this are nearly impossible to produce in most cases.

Leveraging technology for scale

I meet and talk with hundreds of business owners every year and they fall into one of two camps: those who embrace and leverage technology and systems to grow at scale, and those who are determined to do things the way they have always done them and fight change. So which one are you?

I always equate this split to competitors in a triathlon race. Everyone sets off at the same time. They complete the 1.5km swim, then head off on the 10km run. At the end of the run, one guy forgets that it's time to get on the bike for the 40km bike race. He didn't get the memo that it was time to get on the bike, so he just thinks he can keep on running. But even if he runs harder and faster than he has ever run in his life, he will never get close to those who got on the bike.

The same has happened in the business world. A memo should have gone out that you need to run your business like a tech business, a media business or a data business. If you are not on the bike and embracing technology, you can work as hard as you like, but you will never catch the people who are using technology and automation.

I hear it all the time from business owners, how they are working harder than they have ever worked and are not even getting close to their competitors anymore. The businesses who are on the bike and embracing systems are using less effort and less energy than they ever have, and they are growing faster than they ever did before.

In a triathlon it's very clear when to get on the bike, but in business no one sends out a memo to say stop running so hard and get on the bike. So I am sending you that memo now: 'Stop running so hard and get on the bike.'

A recent HubSpot survey revealed that the average mid-sized business uses 198 separate pieces of software, apps and tools. I know that building a system is hard; the challenge faced by businesses is the sheer number of apps, software and tools available to them, so it is inevitable that they struggle.

The annual report by chiefmartec.com on the growth of business apps, tools and software demonstrates this challenge. In 2011 there were around 150 different pieces of software that a business could use; by 2020 this had exploded to 8000. It is therefore little surprise that building an effective system and platform is challenging.

Ease of use is non-negotiable

The inescapable truth is that your system is only as good as the data in it. Your priority must be ease of use because if everyone is comfortable using the system, then they will enter the data you need and you can be confident that it is up to date and providing you with a true perspective on what is happening. As soon as it becomes time consuming and complex, people will start to avoid using your system and you will end up with incomplete data.

At present, your business is a small team of three to five people, so business and communication are straightforward. Everyone knows what information they need and where to find it. However, with scale and growth to a team of 10–12 people, this will not be the case, so focus on making the system intuitive to use.

Secondly, as you grow you need to have a process for onboarding new employees onto the system so that they use it. We are back to process here or using an external onboarding firm to ensure that new team members have the context on each element of the new system and fully understand how to use it.

Lastly, as your business and team grow there are simply more touchpoints with prospects and customers that will need tracking and recording accurately. If you are adding functionality such as messenger, chat bots, support tickets and live chat to your system, then you need your team to monitor and respond quickly and efficiently.

The importance of creating a connected system

A symptom of organic business growth is that the software, tools and technology you are using in your business have little structure. Different people will have championed different pieces of software, usually driven by their own agenda (to make their lives a little bit easier) rather than the overall growth of the business.

You are not on your own with this. It is typical that businesses give little thought to ensuring that the different pieces of technology and software they use can 'talk to each other' or sync data between one another. As with all digital transformation, the first pieces of software brought in will be driven by marketing and sales initiatives.

The result is a 'Frankenstein' system of unconnected pieces of software being used by different people in your business. The fact that these systems aren't linked and data is generated in a silo rather than synced across the entire system will prevent what is call 'closed loop reporting'. Simply put, closed loop reporting is the ability to report on everything that is happening in your business from end to end.

I challenge you to try running meaningful reports or dashboards from the system you have at present; it is nearly impossible. I can almost guarantee that you will end up like the millions of other business owners in the UK who are still using an Excel spreadsheet to cobble together some sort of report on the performance of their business, with duplicate data entries, time wasted and scope for errors.

When you change this to a fully connected system with data moving freely across all areas of your business, you can schedule reports to be generated, have metrics for each key function in your business in dashboards and see practically live, at any minute of the day, where you are in your business growth.

In my business I run a high-level 'growth dashboard' of 12 key metrics that tells me exactly how my business is performing at a macro level, then I have micro dashboards reporting on the website analytics, marketing and lead generation, sales and customer acquisition, operational metrics, support and service metrics. This is possible for any business, and when you get this connected system in place, it is a real 'Aha!' moment.

> **Go be remarkable:** Set up your 'growth dashboard' of the eight to ten key metrics that will tell you exactly how your business is performing at a macro level. When you get this right, it will allow you to see where you are practically live.

Your single source of truth to measure, monitor and record every touchpoint

In Chapter 1 we discussed the importance of making every touchpoint you have with your prospects, customers and partners remarkable, and your system is the platform that will enable you to record, measure and monitor this. If you take nothing else away from this book, take action on this one point now. If you run a B2B business, you must put in place a piece of customer relationship management (CRM) software. As I said above, your old database or spreadsheet that you hold so dear is blocking the growth of your business.

There are some superb CRM systems on the market, such as HubSpot, Zoho, Salesforce, Ontraport, Pipedrive and Monday.com, so sign up to a few free trials and get started with one that fits your style of working. I have used the free HubSpot CRM as the core platform for a number of my businesses, so price is not an issue. Get started, you will never look back.

Your CRM will act as your single source of truth that everything flows through; it will keep track of interactions, data and notes about prospects, customers and partners. All of this data is stored centrally and can be accessed by multiple people across the business, so everyone will always have the latest, most up-to-date information on a customer's experience and their journey with you as a business. You will have the ability to align your sales, marketing, customer service, accounting and management functions as your business grows.

An example of this alignment is a potential customer filling out contact information on a form on your website. After a few follow-up emails with a sales rep, you can update the customer's information to reflect what you've learned about their needs and their company. Marketing can then quickly determine how to best appeal to those needs.

Some of these steps are tracked automatically, while other data may be entered manually. Having everything accessible in one system increases efficiency, speeds up communication and improves the user experience of people who interact with your business.

After using a CRM for nearly a decade now, I have seen how they have transitioned from a database of contacts into fully functioning, automated, cloud-based business systems. The power is in the fact that they integrate with multiple other tools and apps, creating the perfect core for you to develop your system from.

A great example of this is HubSpot, which has a suite of tools, or 'Hubs', built around the free CRM software. There are marketing tools, such as a blog, landing pages, forms, calls to action and email automation, and sales tools, such as sales pipelines, meetings tools, email integration for Microsoft 365 and Gmail, chat bots, call handling, meeting notes, cloud document storage, task automation and email sequences. The Service Hub brings support and service tools, chat, tickets and a knowledgebase. The Operations Hub brings custom two-way syncing of data from other pieces of software into HubSpot and vice versa. Finally, the latest CMS Hub allows you to build your website on HubSpot so that your CRM and website are completely connected, allowing you to see exactly when someone visits your website and what they do there and to engage with them in real time.

I am sure you can see the power of this single source of truth approach and how you can move from not knowing to knowing everything you need to know. This will enable you to have a relevant contextual conversation with your buyers as they move along their buying journey to becoming a customer and also to measure every interaction and put in place metrics at key points to see what is working and what is not.

Enabling data driven decision-making

The one thing we are all good at as business owners is having opinions on our business and what is working and what is not. Unfortunately, we are rarely correct and, to make matters worse, we have a habit of lying to ourselves about how well things are going or to justify a decision we have taken. However, what does not lie is the marketplace. It is brutally honest about how well you are doing and the data will tell you in black and white, no matter what your opinion is.

As we discussed above when looking at developing a single source of truth, a great system will allow you to measure everything, from the core metrics we set out in our strategy that are connected to our overall business growth KPIs down to the contribution each team in our business is making to the overall achievement of those goals.

The more data you can report on in dashboards and physical reports, the more you are armed with the right information to make important decisions as you grow.

At the top level you need to know that you are on track with the revenue being generated by the business and where that revenue is coming from.

You need to know that marketing is generating enough leads for the sales team and where those leads are coming from.

You need to know that your website is working and your target audience is consuming your content.

You need to know that your sales team is making the right number of calls, sending the right level of emails out, having enough meetings and making enough presentations to win new business for you. Sales activity is everything, hence the importance of the LAPS report I discussed in the last chapter on process.

Your sales process is a great example of this in action. If you have a strong CRM, you can use lists for segmentation, create Target Account lists and use lead scoring to identify the best-fit prospects – i.e., prospects that are in the right industry, asking the right questions, consuming the right content and clearly showing intent to buy. You can also identify if they fit your Primary Buyer Persona and are in a position to make the decision or influence a decision-making group. All this enables you to know that your sales team are spending time talking to an active buyer who has a high chance of converting rather than a passive buyer who may buy in the future. Imagine how different your business would be if they were the only people you spoke to on a daily basis.

By using your system in the right way, you have managed to cut out 60% of the time that you or your sales team waste in a day, allowing you to focus on helping the right people, at the right time, with the right information. This is the power of a great system.

In Chapter 10, I will dig deeply into the metrics you need to measure in each area. But for now, let's focus on building a system that measures everything and then decide which data we need to report on and run our dashboards around.

Summary

As with processes allowing you to optimise what you do, procedure by procedure, you need to embrace technology and have a system of tools at the heart of your business that you can leverage to drive growth and scale.

I would go so far as to say that, without having a system around which you build everything in your business, you will struggle to grow predictably. It is as important as creating an effective growth strategy, as it will enable you to execute that strategy and measure the impact of your strategic thinking so you can focus all your time on the things that are working and improving them to make them work better. You will quickly see what is not working and stop doing those things, then you will see the things that need doing to optimise other areas of the business. These are fundamental to predictable growth.

I know it sounds like a lot of work, but it will be a pivotal point in your drive to seven figures and beyond.

Exercise #4 – Audit your tech stack

A tech stack is the tools, software, apps and technology that your business is using. Before you start to develop your new system, take an audit of every piece of software, tool and app you use in your business. Are they easy to use? How many of them are connected and talk to each other? Does your tech stack act as your single source of truth? Does it measure and report on everything? How much are you spending? Are you duplicating functionality? Is there a better way to achieve the outcome?

Bonus task – Shortlist three CRMs to test out and see which one you like.

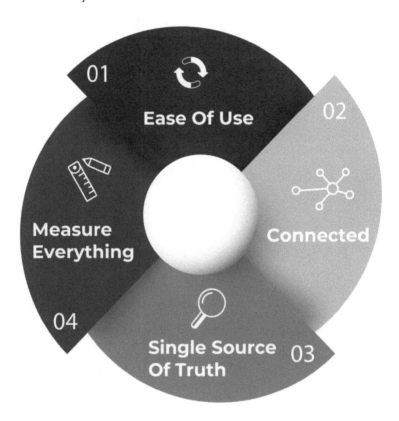

Part 2
Remarkable execution – The STEPS Growth Method

A little about the STEPS Growth Method before I get started with our work together creating your growth strategy. The STEPS methodology is a set of proven principles and processes for growing any B2B business. The focus is on five key elements: Strategy, Traffic, Engagement, Promoters and Systems. I will run through each of these in detail shortly.

There were three reasons why I created this step-by-step methodology to grow a business:

1. I am a serial entrepreneur who has set up and run eight businesses over the past 30 years. In that time, I have learnt what works, what is simply noise and what doesn't work. I feel that every business has taught me valuable lessons that I have carried forward into the next, and this experience has been invaluable.

2. In those 30 years, I have also worked with hundreds of business owners on their own business growth: planning out strategies, developing marketing campaigns, creating content, using social media in the right way, mapping out step-by-step sales processes and using technology to pull it all together.

3. Finally, I have witnessed the impact of technology, the internet, and digital and social media on the way we all make buying decisions. It is crucial that we re-align how we all do business, especially in the B2B world, so that we market and sell in line with how our buyer wants to research and buy.

All this experience has given me a unique skill set and the ability to be able to identify opportunities for growth that many business owners do not see in their own business, as they are so involved in the day-to-day running of it.

It was also clear that there was a pattern to my own successful businesses and those I had worked on with clients. I set about looking at the key elements that B2B business owners needed to get right to become remarkable and would inevitably ensure that they grow to seven figures and beyond.

Above all, as discussed in Chapter 2, I wanted STEPS to be all about remarkable execution in a systematic step-by-step way so that it would both uncover what needed to be done and focus the owner on how to do it.

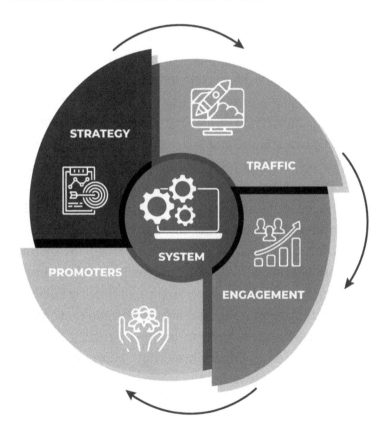

The STEPS Growth Method moves you systematically through five key principles and processes that overcome all the challenges and mistakes you may be making as you grow:

- **Strategy** – First, you will put in place a structured growth strategy that will identify the right target audience for your business, a narrow-focused list of target buyers, and the key tactics to focus on to connect and engage these companies and people. The strategy should then focus on turning them into customers and delighting those customers while putting in place metrics to measure each of these to ensure that you consistently hit your milestones and revenue goals.

- **Traffic** – You will identify the key traffic and lead generation sources that will attract your target audience and good fit buyers to the business. When you know who you are targeting and on what platforms, you can develop marketing campaigns that will put in place a scalable strategy of traffic generation that drives a constant stream of leads into the business.

- **Engagement** – Now you have a predictable stream of leads coming into your business, the process of remarkable engagement kicks in. The highly personalised nurturing of each of your leads via email, the sharing of insights and content, engagement on social media and more traditional outreach are all aimed at building a strong relationship and helping them to move along their buying journey and make a decision. You can help this by giving them the right information at the right time, answering all their questions and naturally converting them into customers and revenue.

- **Promoters** – The secret sauce in the STEPS Growth Method is the focus on remarkable post-sale client engagement. You will put in place processes to deliver your product, service or solution in a way that will delight your customers. But alongside that delivery, you will unlock the full value that these happy clients provide, including developing processes for cross sell and upsell opportunities, sending surveys, requesting reviews, testimonials and case studies and, of course, asking for referrals as a matter of course, not just when someone in your business remembers.

- **Systems** – The final phase is all about developing a remarkable system to pull it all together in your business. I say this is the final phase, but it is something that is ongoing as you move through the other steps in the methodology. You will build a system that is easy to use, fully connected, acts as a single source of truth and measures everything to enable you to make data driven decisions rather than decisions based on your opinion. You will leverage these decisions and your system to grow and scale predictably.

The one thing I want you to take away is that this is hard, focused work. Do it once and do it well and, after the initial period of implementing the STEPS methodology, I am confident that any B2B business owner, no matter where they are now or what sector they work in, will have in place the key elements of a remarkable seven-figure growth plan that will take them to £1m and beyond.

So let's get started.

5. STEPS: Principle 1 – Strategy, Phase 1

Creating your remarkable growth strategy

I originally wrote the strategy execution section as a single chapter. However, as you can see, it ended up being split into two chapters: Phase 1 and Phase 2 of development. It is little surprise, really, as I spend three to four months developing a growth strategy with a client. So when I speak to business owners and they say something along the lines of 'I sat down on Sunday evening to work on my strategy' or 'I have a business plan that we review once a year', it is hard not to roll my eyes or ask them how that is working out for them.

In STEPS, the strategy planning phase has evolved over the past ten years. As the world has changed, I have added new elements and removed others that were no longer having the impact I demand from this methodology. It is critical to me that the methodology evolves as the B2B business world evolves.

When you start planning out your strategy, it is important to break it down into 12 key elements. Each of these has a pivotal role in your business growth, so spend at least a week on each to ensure that the level of detail and depth will take out any guesswork when you come to executing and implementing the strategy.

The 12 key elements are:

- Objectives, targets and goals – Focused on revenue growth
- Target market – The who – Sectors, companies and people
- Positioning – Our brand, colours, fonts, logo, tagline, culture, mission, vision and origin story
- The market and competitors – Competition analysis and understanding of opportunities
- Product/service/solution development plan – The what of our offering
- Sales plan – Revenue and customer goals, sales process and pipeline management
- Marketing plan – Lead generation campaigns, content, social media and sales enablement

- Talent and recruitment plan
- Operational delivery
- Service and support
- Systems development
- Metrics, analytics and reporting

It's all about revenue growth

As you can see, the STEPS approach to strategy creation is all about growth. It focuses on driving predictable revenue growth and building the structure in the business to deliver that growth. The model is built on you understanding who is a 'good fit' and who is a 'bad fit' for what you do.

You are positioning your business with crystal clarity in the market. Your position is 'This is who we help, this is the problem we help them overcome, this is how we do it and this is why we are better than anyone else at doing it'.

Setting your strategic objectives

If you completed the exercise at the end of Chapter 2, you already have some top-line objectives, a revenue goal and key metrics to measure as you execute your growth strategy.

I also want you to take the time to consider the impact on your business as you start to hit these goals. You will need to expand your team, have access to more resources and bring in more diverse skill sets, so give some thought to this now.

Importantly, think about how you are going to align everyone in your business around the achievement of these goals. This is a team sport and everyone needs to play their part. The business owner who tries to impose their strategy on the rest of the team will struggle, as people will not feel part of the journey or invested in the mission and vision of the business.

I share some ideas on this final point in Chapter 12, including approaches I have seen work really well such as holding a strategy launch day with your entire team.

Identifying your target market

As you will see when we discuss positioning, the importance of narrowing down who your best customer is and understanding them better than they understand themselves is critical to your business growth.

Start by auditing the past 100 orders or customers that you have dealt with, then answer these seven questions:

- Can you identify a sector or industry that purchased from you more than any other?
- Who had the most success by using your service, product or solution?
- Who did you enjoy working with and who did you not enjoy working with?
- What size company were they – small, mid or corporate?
- Geographically, where were they based?
- How many employees did they have?
- What was their turnover?

Identify your ICP

By identifying the answers to the seven questions above, you will have an accurate **Ideal Customer Profile (ICP)** for your 'good fit' customers and prospective new customers.

Now you know your ICP and sector, you can quickly build out a **Target List** of all the companies within that sector that fit your criteria. Whether they currently work with you or not is irrelevant.

List all of the **Companies** in this sector – i.e., there may be 300–400 companies who fit your criteria. Then I recommend you take one more step and split these companies into tiers – i.e., Tier 1 companies are the top 10% in that sector, Tier 2 are the next 40%, and Tier 3 are the bottom 50%. You can categorise your tiers by revenue or size of the business, depending on what is most important to you. You will see why this is so crucial as we roll out our marketing campaigns.

Identify your Primary Buyer Personas

Now think of the **people** who work in those companies. In a business-to-business decision-making process, it is normal for four to five people to be involved, especially for a larger, considered purchase that may require sign-off from the finance director or senior management.

Think back to meetings you have been involved with and identify your **Primary Buyer Persona (PBP)**. This is usually the champion who you met with – the person you initially speak to and gets the conversation moving in their organisation. Think about their daily responsibilities and challenges and how you can help them succeed in their role. If you focus on making their life easier, you will soon have them onside.

Your PBP will be the person you want to attract and focus your effort on at this stage, but, over time, it is perfectly normal to build out a number of personas for your business for the entire decision-making group, including potential blockers and the information they will need.

Map out a persona profile and ask yourself these questions in four key areas to really understand them:

- What are their **demographics**? Keep this simple – gender, age, education, marital status, number of children, income and geography.
- How do they make decisions? Think through their **psychographics**. This is how they make a buying decision and will include their interests, priorities, values, personality type, i.e., profile, payoffs and prizes, mistakes they are making and challenges they are facing.
- Next, think about their **role**. What is it and what does it involve? What do they do on a daily basis in their job? How are they measured? What are their responsibilities and what is the pain that they will be getting a solution for?
- Finally, think about their **sources of information**. What are their trusted sources of information? What blogs do they read? What influencers do they follow? What is their go-to social media platform, their favourite sources of news, their favourite websites, magazines or printed media? And, finally, what trade shows or events do they attend?

As part of this section of the strategy, you must map out the buying journey they go on when they make a buying decision. Maybe keep it simple for now, but evolve it over time. I would start with three stages broken down into:

The Awareness Stage – When they first realise they have a problem, challenge or opportunity, they will most likely do general research to understand and define the problem in front of them.

The Consideration Stage – Once they understand and have defined the problem, they will move onto more detailed research to refine their options for a solution. The goal here is to build a shortlist of possible solutions and companies who can offer the answer to their problem.

The Decision Stage – Now they will use reviews, trials and conversations with the company to select the person they want to deal with. Generally, it is at this stage of the journey that they will reach out and make contact with most businesses.

I hope you can see why going deep here is so critical to your growth. By doing this strategic work, you will know exactly how to attract the right audience and what content to produce for different stages of their buying journey, and you will be able to determine active buyers with a genuine intent to buy from the content they consume and the questions they ask.

You can also position yourself as the expert and thought-leader in the mind of these people, giving you a significant advantage over your competition, as you understand the persona better than anyone else.

Go be remarkable: Conduct persona interviews. The work of persona development and understanding your personas is not limited to your strategy creation. It should be an ongoing task, and the deeper your

> understanding of your persona, the more effective you will be at helping them. A persona interview is when you identify 10–15 customers who fit your Primary Buyer Persona and interview them, asking some of the questions above and digging into their buying journey to have a greater understanding. You can then use your CRM to ensure your entire team has access to this evolving information. This is truly a sign of a remarkable business.

Understanding the market

I want you to do some deep work here on understanding your potential market size and the size of the opportunity you have for your business. Now you have defined your ICP, define your Total Addressable Market (TAM) size, what other markets you can expand into, and who your competitors are, locally, nationally and globally. If you have broken the market down into tiers, you can now start to build out your Target Account List (TA) of all the potential customers you need to connect and engage with. It does not matter if you work with them or not at this stage.

Clarifying your positioning – be a specialist not a generalist

The number one mistake that I see with B2B businesses is that they go too broad and become regarded as a generalist. The problem with being a generalist is that you are seen as a jack of all trades and master of none, so, while you are kidding yourself that you sell to everyone, you are selling to no one. The main issue with this is that, when the market is dealing with generalists, it has no unique value attached to your offering and will always come down to price.

The secret to success is to go narrow, position yourself as a specialist and dominate a very specific position in the market. If you are serious about getting to seven figures, you must stop trying to offer everything to everyone and focus on being the best at solving one problem for one person better than anyone else.

I want you to remember that you will still attract other business as you market and raise awareness of what you do, but it is important to take a position in the market and establish yourself as an expert and thought-leader. When you take this position, people will want to work with you and price will be secondary.

Building out your product offerings

At present you probably think you have one core service or maybe a few products that you are selling as a business, but a remarkable business will build out a product ecosystem that engages their target market, converts website visitors into leads, has a clearly defined core offering for people to get started working with them and then additional upsell and cross sell products to offer to customers. These build multiple streams of income, and each serves an important role in the growth of your business.

As you develop your strategy and grow the business, it is natural for your products, services and solutions to develop, and these will generally fall into four categories:

- Free products
- Conversion products
- Core product
- Upsell/cross sell products

Each of these will be expanded on in the following chapters, as the first two fall into sales and marketing, the third into operational delivery and the final products are for existing customers and promoters of your business. I will address each in the relevant phase of the STEPS process, for context.

Exercise #5 – Create your Primary Buyer Persona

Download the Buyer Persona worksheet from www.goberemarkable.com/resources to start creating your Primary Buyer Persona. This may be the first of many, but it should be your best buyer now so that you understand the demographics, or who they are, and the psychographics of how they make buying decisions.

Answer the questions with data wherever possible or make calculated guesses, then mature this into more accurate information by talking to your sales team and doing the buyer persona interviews I suggested with existing customers who fit the profile.

6. STEPS: Principle 1 – Strategy, Phase 2

The unstoppable sales plan – predictable customer acquisition

Although lead generation comes before customer acquisition in the traditional funnel, when planning your strategy I recommend completing your sales plan first. The reason for this is that your sales plan will dictate your revenue goals for the year ahead and define how many leads you need marketing to generate and the campaigns that will need to be run through your marketing plan.

Download the Sales Plan Planner in the resources section[6] to plan out your sales revenue goals, which products this revenue is coming from and what actions you need to take to hit these goals.

Set up an inbound sales process

The key to predictable revenue is to create a high-converting inbound sales process that every lead goes through. This needs to be replicable by the entire sales team and easy to understand for new sales people joining the team.

As leads are handed over from your marketing team, these will be classed as a Marketing Qualified Lead (MQL) – that is to say, they hit all the criteria you have set for a lead. Now the sales team (or you) take over and start nurturing them into Sales Qualified Leads (SQLs) – do they tick all the boxes you need to tick to be able to convert them into a sales opportunity and ultimately a sale?

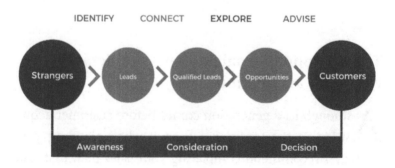

Inbound Sales Methodology

---

[6] www.goberemarkable.com/resources

The four-stage inbound sales process I recommend you start with is **Identify, Connect, Explore, Advise.**

Every industry will have slight variations, but this principle applies across the board and it will stop your sales team rushing the process, ensuring that each lead is dealt with in a predictable manner that aligns with the way the buyer makes a natural buying decision and addresses all their questions or objections as they move along it.

Identify – Develop a 'Good Fit Matrix' to determine that each lead ticks all of your criteria. If you have done the work I recommended on the six or seven criteria to identify your Ideal Customer Profile, then this should be a binary 'yes' or 'no'; they either fit the criteria of a target company or not.

Then you move onto the contact or person themselves. Do they fit your Primary Buyer Persona criteria and is their activity consistent with someone who is actively in a buying cycle? Finally, from the content they have consumed or actions they have taken so far, work out where they are in the buying journey so you can keep your conversations relevant and helpful.

Remember, your CRM should allow you to score all of these areas, and if you are using a system such as HubSpot, you can actually automate your lead scoring to make this a straightforward process and ensure your sales team are only talking to the top 20 warmest leads at any one time to move them along the process. Do your research on them before reaching out and connecting.

Connect – Now you have identified that the lead is a good fit, the right person and actively in a buying cycle, you can move onto connecting with them.

The process here is to make the connection natural but effective. If they were an inbound lead that visited your website and completed a form, then do some research on them and follow up their interest with a phone call, then an email and then a further call, if you did not get through the first time.

The important part of the connect stage is a good follow-up technique and cadence. Most sales people give up after the first attempt – don't do this. When you do get to speak to the person, keep it brief: the maximum is 15 minutes for the connect call. This call is all about them and their world, not you. You need to understand their situation, ask questions and listen.

Go be remarkable: I recommend always connecting with them on LinkedIn first. Do some research on them, visit their website and find something to talk about – i.e., an award they won, where they live or went to school/university; on the company website, look for awards that the business has won or milestones they have reached. Then connect on LinkedIn and mention the research you have done, i.e., 'Hi John. I was just on your website and saw you had won the Best East Midlands Business award – great work. Thought I would reach out and connect on LinkedIn. Have a good day. Richard'. As you can see, this is non-threatening and non-sales focused and it works brilliantly. They will also recognise you when you call.

Explore – Once you have had the initial call with the prospect, you will have talked about their challenges and what they are looking to achieve and built a little rapport, so now it is time to dive deeper into the issues raised, what to consider and possible solutions.

You must do this in a separate exploratory call, as this will probably last around an hour. You also need to ensure that all the people involved in the decision-making process are present on the call.

Make sure you set an agenda, recap what was discussed in the initial call, then work through a planned presentation deck to ensure that your exploratory calls are consistent every time. What you are identifying here is if you have a solution to their problem, so make sure you spend the time exploring everything you need to know to decide if you can help. Only in the last five to ten minutes do you talk about yourself and your solution.

Advise – Now is the time for you to present your solution, pricing and next steps and get sign-off from the prospect. This may be a face-to-face presentation to a group or a Zoom call, but, again, make sure you have a polished deck that is personal to those in attendance and recaps the problems, some of the mistakes that are being made and then the solution, how the solution will be delivered and the outcome of using the solution. Be specific here with your outcome.

At Digital Media Edge our presentation deck had three outcomes clearly defined – a worst-case scenario, an expected scenario and a best-case scenario – each one with traffic, leads and sales clearly listed. We left no grey area here. We then launched into the pricing and next steps.

I hope this makes sense to you and you look at your own sales process and adapt it. The biggest mistake I see in B2B sales is that the sales person is so excited to get their prospect on the phone that they try to sell everything in one call, totally overwhelming the prospect with information over-load and blowing what could have been a great opportunity. If you take it slowly, avoid any type of pressure and make it a natural sales conversation that has logical next steps, then your sales conversion percentage will go through the roof.

Set up your sales pipeline

As far as your CRM is concerned, you now need to map these four stages of your sales process into your sales pipeline. At the start of your pipeline you need Marketing Qualified Leads (MQLs) for all the leads that are handed over from marketing to sales, then at the end of the pipeline you need columns for Closed/Lost and Closed/Won to track all deals through.

Go be remarkable: Create a Closed/Lost Process. Closed/Lost is vital to track as you can then set up an automated process of following these up after 4, 8 and 12 weeks. In my experience, you will get up to 20% of these deals back in by setting up this single process, if done correctly.

Sales enablement

In modern B2B businesses, the marketing and sales functions are becoming de-siloed and the line between the two is less defined, as aligning the two teams around revenue is far more beneficial to the overall efficiency of your marketing and sales 'machine'.

In his book *Inbound Organization*, Dan Tyre coined the phrase 'Smarketing' to sum up this modern approach to lead generation and customer acquisition. Sales enablement is all about creating a feedback loop between marketing and sales, where marketing is tasked with generating leads but also with supporting the nurturing of those leads by creating content, social media posting, blog posting and videos to support the sales team as they move a prospective customer along the buying journey.[7]

My advice is that you strategically plan now for this to happen. It makes total sense that your sales team are at the sharp end talking to customers and prospects every day. They will hear the same questions day in and day out, so, by holding monthly Smarketing meetings and encouraging them to capture these questions and feed them back to the marketing team, they can be addressed in content that can be shared by the sales team and added to the knowledgebase. This is being buyer centric and listening to what the buyer is telling you.

The remarkable marketing plan – Your lead generation machine

Your marketing plan is all about lead generation, or how you will attract your target audience to your website and convert them from visitors into leads in your CRM.

Your marketing plan will be campaign driven and involve creating a range of campaign assets for each campaign. The most important assets will be your content assets, but the work you have done on your Primary Buyer Persona and Ideal Customer Profile will now help you develop your

---

[7] D. Tyre and T. Hockenberry, *Inbound Organization* (2018).

content strategy. You can develop content and insights by answering the questions your buyers are asking at each stage of their journey, so by aligning your marketing with each stage of their buying journey. These assets will include guides, reports, white papers, checklists, videos, blog posts, case studies, testimonials and infographics.

Which type of B2B marketing campaign should you choose?

Most B2B businesses will suit one or both of the following types of marketing campaign: inbound marketing or account-based marketing (ABM)

I find that, for most B2B businesses, a mix of the two works best, with inbound marketing creating a volume of leads and ABM being a more highly targeted approach to attracting specific people from specific high-value accounts. I will quickly cover both approaches so that you can decide which is most appropriate for your business and current position or use both.

Inbound Marketing – As opposed to traditional outbound marketing, where you broadcast at people and hope a few become aware of what you do, inbound is all about sharing valuable content to connect and engage with your persona. The content is usually educational or solution content in the form of blog posts, videos and social media posts that address problems, answer questions or generally help. These then encourage the persona to visit your website, where they consume more content and exchange their contact details for a conversion offer to become a lead. Inbound is all about creating remarkable content.

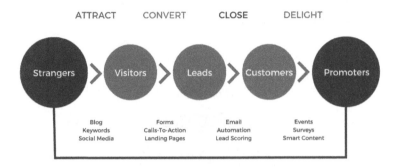

Inbound Marketing Methodology

ATTRACT   CONVERT   CLOSE   DELIGHT

Strangers > Visitors > Leads > Customers > Promoters

Blog	Forms	Email	Events
Keywords	Calls-To-Action	Automation	Surveys
Social Media	Landing Pages	Lead Scoring	Smart Content

Account-Based Marketing – ABM is all about identifying the high-value accounts in your target sector, using highly targeted, personalised outreach to specific people within specific companies, then engaging with people who respond and show intent. I always equate ABM to developing a standalone marketing strategy to attract the attention of each individual high-value account.

In every sector there are tiers of companies. Think about the engineering sector, for example. This is a huge sector in the UK, with thousands of engineering companies. Now, you could target all of those companies, or your strategy may be to only target the top Tier 1 companies such as Siemens. You can see here the difference between inbound marketing, where you would develop marketing campaigns to attract anyone in the engineering sector, and an ABM campaign that would focus on the top 5% of engineering businesses, a small but very lucrative market if you were to get a contract with one of these Tier 1 companies. In the 'Account-Based Marketing Methodology' diagram, you can see how, in ABM, you create a small, focused Target Account List, expand this into multiple contacts within each company on your Target Account List, then have multiple touchpoints with each contact and create advocates.

Account-Based Marketing Methodology

Account Selection	Identify	Target Account List
Contact Identification	Expand	Personas / Personalisation
Relationship Nurture	Engage	Email / LinkedIn / Content
Account Conversion	Advocate	Create Opportunity

Adding social media to your marketing mix

Again, the work you have done on your Primary Buyer Persona will pay dividends here, as you will know what social media platform to focus on. Your target B2B audience will be on LinkedIn, with some Twitter posting required for tapping into the sector and community and YouTube for video content.

Using paid marketing campaigns to drive traffic volume

The most scalable form of marketing is paid campaigns. You can set these up and literally turn them on and off when you want more or fewer leads to be generated. As long as you are measuring your return on investment (ROI) and you know metrics such as your Cost of Customer Acquisition (COCA) and Customer Lifetime Value (CLV), they are incredibly valuable. I would recommend testing Google AdWords and LinkedIn Campaigns for maximum ROI. They give instant results and will complement your organic marketing campaigns to hit those lead goals you have set yourself.

Traditional marketing

In B2B marketing, it is still important not to forget trade events, shows and industry magazines for print advertising. In certain sectors, you can still generate great awareness and leads from these more traditional sources, although measuring them and getting accurate ROI figures is more difficult, and it can be an expensive route compared to digital marketing efforts.

Talent and recruitment plan

An area of growth strategy planning with clients that has developed and evolved over the past few years has been in recruitment and how the owner builds a team around themselves. Many businesses have grown organically and taken people on to do various roles in the business, basically filling seats as needed, as opposed to focusing on the key roles that need filling at the right time.

As you grow you will be building your team, and you must focus on building a culture that attracts the very best talent to your business.

Your first 10–12 hires, after you and your business partner, will probably look something like this:

- **Sales Manager** – Initially, your first hire must be focused on sales and business development. I have learnt this lesson many times and pass it on to you for free. You must invest in a first-class sales professional who has the potential to develop into a sales manager and probably a sales director down the line, so spend around £35k+ on this person.

- **Sales Executive x2** – This will give you a sales team of three eventually and in B2B you need this – again, to avoid you being on the road selling all the time.
- **Marketing Executive and Content Writer** – These must excel at content creation. I would look for a journalism student for this role and teach them the marketing side.
- **Social Media Executive and Graphic Designer** – They must be comfortable with graphic design, animation and video editing software.
- **Operations Executive x2** – This will remove the majority of the delivery from you, but you can still manage this side and touch base with clients regularly.
- **Service and Support Executive** – It is crucial to have someone in this role whose goal is not just to handle support queries but to develop the customer relationship and account manage.
- **Finance/Accounts Executive** – This does not need to be a senior finance director yet, but someone with accountancy training who can manage all the day-to-day finances and compliance.
- **IT/Tech Support** – As you build out your system, having someone on your team who has technical skills is invaluable, especially when it comes to cyber security and cyber essentials knowledge.

Yes, some of the above roles and functions could be outsourced, but eventually having them in-house will give you greater flexibility and resources as you scale.

Go be remarkable: Only recruit A-players. When you recruit, you must look for the best in each role. Do not try to hire a B- or a C-player when an A-player will deliver 150% more; it is false economy. Pay what it takes to get that team of A-players in your business and you will not look back.

The secret to effective modern recruitment is that it is rarely about money anymore: it is about career choices, and especially for Gen Z and younger students/graduates. They have different agendas and are making decisions based on culture, social responsibility, purpose, sustainability and companies who work with charities and for good, outside of profit.

So make sure, as part of your recruitment, that you talk about career paths and opportunities in the future.

Talk about your culture and share stories of life working in your business that inspire.

Talk about your vision, mission and origin story. Talk about the values of your business. Share your induction pack and discuss how you will support them with regular reviews and appraisals.

Share your social purpose and responsibility and even your sustainability policy. I heard a story recently from an accountant friend of mine who was interviewing a young graduate for a position in the firm and the interviewee asked about the company's social purpose and sustainability policy, including what they had in place to become carbon neutral. She disclosed that, in the previous interview she had with a rival firm, they had shared this freely with her. I think this underlines that this was an important part of her decision on which to join. Share work you are doing for good other than just making profit, such as charities you support and events you run that raise money for good causes.

Lastly, and most importantly, make sure you onboard new team members properly with a structured training, coaching and mentoring approach over the initial three months so that you build up their confidence and competence systematically, then give them the tools to succeed. But more on that later.

Delightful operational delivery

I will not spend too much time on your operational delivery strategy, as every business will have a different product, service or solution as their core offering, but I will emphasise that, when looking at what and how you deliver, you must focus on making it remarkable and delighting your customers time after time.

The one thing I will repeat, though, is that you need to release yourself as quickly as possible from this area of the business so that you can focus on the high-value strategic work of growth. Therefore, make this one of your priorities in the first iteration of the strategy. I meet so many owners who have not taken this step and are stuck delivering to clients years later.

Your time is better spent on developing the product ecosystem and driving the business forward towards that seven-figure goal.

Your core product, service or solution is your starting point here, so put in place metrics that can measure delivery of this.

Do you need to develop a more transparent onboarding of clients so they know exactly what to expect when they work with your business? I found that working out a process for mapping out the first 90 days working with any client worked brilliantly for Digital Media Edge. We literally broke down week by week what the first 12 weeks of working with us looked like. I have done this in a number of my businesses and clients always loved it.

Focus groups and surveys are another key part of this. Regularly getting together small groups of customers to feed back on how you can improve and innovate your core product offering is helpful – and the more honest they are, the better for you. Also set up a repeatable process for sending every client a survey asking five to ten questions aimed at improving your operational delivery. I go into detail on this in Chapter 9 when we talk about client engagement.

Remarkable service and support

The natural run on from delivering your services remarkably is to listen to customers' problems and support them as they use your core product or service.

You must have someone in your organisation who is accountable for this part of the business. Give them tools to help them succeed, such as setting up a digital ticketing system on a Twitter feed for support queries. Allow them to monitor mentions across social media so that, when anyone mentions the business, they can respond quickly.

Set up a support email that is solely for clients, customers and their questions.

Set up a knowledgebase of the most commonly asked questions with articles and videos. Also think about a resources area on your website for this, too.

Give the responsibility for producing your customer newsletter to the service and support executive. This is positive news and they can work with marketing to make it relevant and interesting.

Ensure your service and support executive is responsible for generating reviews, testimonials and case studies – again, working with marketing and feeding back comments from happy customers. This needs to be processed out and become part of your strategy.

Finally, I recommend you start recording progress by tracking your Net Promoter Score (NPS) to gauge customer satisfaction and the likelihood of them recommending you to other people.

Systems development

The final part of your strategy needs to revolve around building your systems and technology up in a structured way so that you have the business data you need to make decisions and your team has the tools and apps they need to leverage to excel in their roles. I go into detail in Chapter 10, but, for your strategy work, map out what you need your system to do, what you have now and identify the best way to connect it all together.

Your strategic approach to system development will revolve around the following:

Core platform build

As discussed in Chapter 4, this will revolve around developing a customer relationship management (CRM) system that everyone in the business uses and that tracks every interaction you have with prospects, leads, companies and partners, allowing you to make informed decisions and keep the conversation relevant.

Website development

Your website is an integral part of your system, so don't just treat it as a marketing task. Make getting it right a priority from a strategic point of view.

We are going to embrace a growth-driven design approach that will be developed and improved every quarter, to turn it from a 'brochure' site that does little but talk about your business, your services, your team and your products into a buyer-centric site that positions you as a specialist in the visitor's challenges, shares valuable content and insights, and builds a community. Your website needs to be focused on the user experience as well as mobile optimised, secure, fast and valuable to the visitors. Your website should include a blog, a resources area and chat bots with live chat to help people find what they need quickly and at any time of the day. I cover this in detail in Chapter 10.

Marketing tools

Your system should incorporate the critical tools for your marketing team – such as blogging, social media management, landing pages, paid ad management, calls to action, forms, email automation and campaign management – so that they can attract and convert visitors into leads.

Sales tools

Ensure your sales team has email integration, lead scoring, documents, a knowledgebase, meetings, automated email sequences, video outreach and pipeline automation so that it can identify the most engaged leads and convert them into customers and revenue.

Operations tools

These integrate with your operations software and allow you to report and sync data from your operational delivery such as ERP, WMS and LMS platforms.

Service tools

Ensure that the service team has a robust ticketing system, email integration, tasks, notifications, support bots, social media messenger and automation to enable any customer query to be dealt with promptly.

Analytics tools

Finally, make sure you can measure everything so you know exactly what is working and why, from website analytics to marketing ROI and sales conversions. This all relies on you putting together a connected system that will allow easy reporting on all aspects of your growth plan.

Metrics, analytics and reporting

The final part of your strategy should break down your key metrics, what dashboards need setting up and how you are going to report on them. The key here is to identify the metrics that are important or the metrics that matter. I look at the importance of differentiating between lead, current and lag metrics in Chapter 10.

As you develop your initial strategy, focus on ten key metrics for each of the following areas:

Core business growth metrics

This will be led by your revenue goal and reverse engineered from there, as you did in Chapter 2. You should have a dashboard and a report of eight to ten metrics.

Marketing/lead generation metrics

There are ten metrics that measure how well you are doing here – again, number of new leads in the CRM is your lead metric, then a lead source report, website traffic, landing pages, blog posts, email performance, i.e., number sent, number opened, etc., then MQLs, which may be different from the number of leads.

A quick word of warning here. Do not measure 'vanity metrics' such as number of followers or likes on social media: these are totally irrelevant. Focus on engagement and views of videos for re-marketing lists and audiences, as these are valuable. You are focusing on lead generation and ROI with your marketing, so you need to understand what is working and what to invest more into.

Sales metrics

Again, focus on ten metrics for sales that will accurately tell you how well your sales process is working. I recommend focusing on activity as the lead metrics – calls, emails, meetings and presentations held each week. In every business I have worked in and with, the most active sales people are the ones who hit their targets and excel. Also focus on conversion rates at each stage of the pipeline/process. Where are the blocks and what needs improving?

Operational delivery

Identify any key metrics for the delivery of your product. What are the ways you can measure if you are delivering remarkably to your clients?

Service and support

Monitor metrics such as number of support tickets, response times and your Net Promoter Score (NPS).

Summary

I hope this has given you an overview of how to put together a remarkable growth strategy, one that is going to ensure that everything you and your team work on daily will be driving you towards seven figures and becoming a truly remarkable business. As I said at the start of Chapter 5, I make no apology that this chapter and the previous one have been as deep as they have. This is going to give you every chance of making it a success and thinking strategically about the growth of your business.

So focus the next three to six months of your time on getting the 12 pivotal elements we have discussed in this chapter down in your strategy. I recommend developing your strategy in a lever arch file, with dividers, to allow you to review and revise it each year based on your previous year's performance.

Then make sure you communicate it and align your entire business around it; get the buy in of all the key stakeholders and everyone in the business. I recommend a quarterly full-team meeting to celebrate the wins, look at where it can be improved and identify areas that are not working.

Go be remarkable: Reward the wins. One of the most powerful concepts I have come across is performance-related rewards. Let everyone know what the revenue goals are for the year. If they exceed these goals as a team, you put 5% of the excess in a pot to reward everyone. I know a recruitment firm in Bristol called ISL that took the whole team away skiing for a long weekend – even people who had just joined the business went on the trip. The social media posts and the culture that this portrayed were incredible. Who would not want to work for a business like that? Can you imagine what that would be like in your business and the talent you would attract?

Exercise #6 – Get started on your strategy planning

I hope that by the time you get to this exercise you have grasped the massive importance of getting your strategy right.

In fact, to underline this, I recommend you do not go any further in the book until you have done this exercise and mapped out the 12 key elements of your growth strategy. Get a lever arch folder and download the Strategy Contents checklist from www.goberemarkable.com/resources, then get started. Your sales plan will really help with this, so download the sales plan document too and get started with this.

7. STEPS: Principle 2 – Traffic

Highly targeted traffic creates highly engaged leads

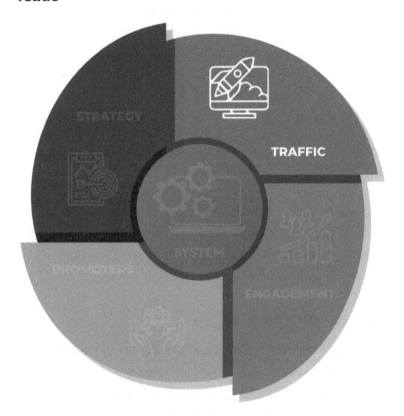

Now you have your strategy in place to give you direction, it is time to start developing the engine room of your business growth, and the first process we need in place is an efficient way of driving a predictable flow of traffic that we can convert into leads.

The work you have done in your strategy on your Ideal Customer Profile, Primary Buyer Persona and Market will be invaluable in your traffic generation, as the goal is not to waste energy, resources and money on attracting anything other than good fit visitors to your website – i.e., people who have a need and can have success with your product, service or solution.

So don't over complicate this. Traffic is abundant, and although marketers, search engine optimisation (SEO) companies and pay-per-click (PPC) agencies like to make out that traffic generation is a dark art, it really isn't, and you will already be doing a lot of it, just maybe not in a highly targeted way.

There are effectively two types of traffic you can generate.

Traffic you control

This will be from paid ads, social media posts, videos, referrals and printed material. It should nearly always be sent to a landing page that has been optimised for conversion and is highly relevant to the visitor.

Traffic you don't control

This will be referred traffic, search traffic or someone typing in your company domain name or company name directly into a browser. This will go to your homepage, so you need to structure your homepage and navigation to allow for this.

Go be remarkable: Don't send traffic to your homepage unless there is no other option. One of my biggest frustrations is when I see how many businesses are still sending traffic to the homepage of their website, then leaving the visitor to find what they want. It is lazy and unhelpful and it damages the user experience of your business so don't do it, especially if you still have a brochure website that has not been conversion optimised.

I talked about having a minimum of a 2% conversion rate of website visitors into leads, and this is achieved by following the simple rule of sending most of the traffic to key landing pages, then offering value and a conversion offer or product that will add more value and capture the visitor's details.

We can break down these types of traffic into three sources.

Organic traffic

This includes direct, earned, referred, email and search engine traffic. Search engine traffic is where the volume will come from predominantly, so investment in SEO is understandable to ensure you are ranking for the right terms and keywords.

Social media traffic

Generated by a regular posting schedule and interesting content mix across LinkedIn, Twitter and YouTube for B2B social success.

Paid ad traffic

Paid ad campaigns will include paid search adverts using Google Ads, re-marketing ads on LinkedIn, Twitter and

YouTube video views, plus highly targeted social media lead generation campaigns on LinkedIn and YouTube. These video ads are run through Google Ads again.

Your strategy will have identified what level of website traffic you need to be getting to generate the leads to hit your goals, so focus on achieving these numbers.

Let's look at each traffic source in turn and what processes we need to put in place.

Organic traffic generation

Every website will generate organic traffic naturally, as people put their website address on their email signatures, social media profiles, business cards and brochures, so this direct traffic will naturally start to flow, albeit to the homepage.

Build out your keyword lists for search engine optimisation (SEO)

When I start working with a client, I always analyse their website using the Ahrefs free site explorer tool. You can use it by simply signing up for their free Webmaster tools.[8]

When you run your website address or domain name through the tool, it will give you a list of the keywords and phrases your website is ranking for in the search engines and what position they are ranking.

The power of this is that you can easily see how people are currently finding you and where your easy opportunities are for improving your ranking and level of traffic from the search engines. You can export this in an Excel or .csv file.

---

[8] www.ahrefs.com

> **Go be remarkable:** Another great website for getting a list of keywords that are question related is www. answerthepublic.com. You can use it to search for any topic and it will pull in lists of questions asked on the subject.

Secondly, get a list of all the questions your sales team hear regularly from customers and prospects, then identify how someone would type this into Google to find the answer. This will give you a list of long-tail keyword phrases that will be lower volume but low competition, too, and that you can rank for easily. Again, this is gold, as any traffic you get from these are likely to be very warm prospects looking for answers to questions.

Finally, do some keyword research yourself into your key topics. I recommend using tools such as Keywords Everywhere,[9] which has a great Chrome extension that will scan any page for keywords. Additionally, the Google Ads Keywords tool and SEM Rush[10] are good keyword research tools.

I tend to do my initial keyword research manually, then use tools to expand the lists. I start by typing in a keyword or longer-tail keyword phrase, then look at the recommendations that Google makes.

I build out a list of keywords, then split them into topics and categories. These will also form the basis of our content planner in the next phase of engagement.

Remember, this is all about thinking like your Primary Buyer Persona: what are their challenges, pains and mistakes,

---

[9] www.keywordseverywhere.com

[10] www.semrush.com

what solutions are they looking for and how would they type it into a search engine to research information. Remember that, in the awareness stage of the journey, they will be using shorter, broader phrases to help them understand their position, then, as they move along into the consideration stage, they will be typing in longer phrases as they get more specific around solutions and refine their search.

Use your blog as a traffic magnet

The biggest asset you can develop for attracting website traffic is the development of your blog and posting on it regularly. I would recommend posting once a week to your blog and focusing your blog content on the keywords you have generated in the previous list.

Focus on creating answers to questions, problems, mistakes and solution content that will be valuable to your Primary Buyer Persona. You know they will be researching these using Google, which loves blog posts and will index each one. Over time this will allow you to build up multiple pieces of content around a topic.

As mentioned, I recommend a cadence of publishing one blog post per week, and give this to your marketing executive as a priority. Do not be tempted to do this yourself, as, while you may be able to do this, it is going to take two to three hours to write a good blog post, and you are better off spending those 12 hours per month elsewhere.

Then make sure you optimise your blog post for the search engines so that when it gets indexed, you start to rise up the rankings.

Go be remarkable: Add strong calls to action (CTA) to your blog posts. Remember that, by finding and reading your blog posts, people are displaying interest and intent, so always have strong calls to actions in your posts. These will be determined by where they are in the buyer's journey, so if it is a top-of-the-funnel type blog post, then offer a PDF or report as a download; if it is a more bottom-of-the-funnel or decision-making stage post, then offer a free consultation or trial. These convert well, as they are relevant to what the visitor has been reading about.

Search engine optimise the core pages, pillar pages and topic clusters on your website

As well as your blog posts being search engine optimised, you need to make sure each of your core website pages are optimised so that they rank in the search engines. So optimise your about page, your services page, your resources pages, your pillar pages and, of course, your homepage.

My advice is to always link out from your blog posts to your core pages, as this will give a strong internal linking structure and rank your core pages well.

Don't forget to write core topic pages called 'pillar pages' around the main subjects you want to be known for. These are usually in excess of 4,000 words and will be the main pages you want to get ranked for in Google. Your blog posts and other pages can then link to these pages and form what are called 'topic clusters'. When you perform a search in Google, you can see how the most relevant authority on a topic is returned as the main snippet. These are pillar pages, and your goal is to rank your pillar page as the main snippet returned for a search on your core topic.

Driving referral traffic

In B2B businesses and sectors there are many ways to get links back to your website. These are valuable for SEO but also send traffic through, so ask for links on:

- Online directories – Yes, people still search Yell and company directories, but you should get listed in Google Business, Yahoo and LinkedIn, too.
- Industry directories – Are there any specific industry or sector directories?
- Industry organisations – What are the big trade organisations in the sector you are targeting and can you get listed in them?
- Industry magazines – These are still a great way to get links back to your website.
- Industry trade shows/exhibitions – Again, these are a great way to be associated with and get traffic from referrals from these shows.

Driving direct traffic

Finally, make sure your website details are everywhere – on every brochure, on your letterhead, on your PowerPoint slide decks, on your business card, on your videos and on your email signature.

Direct traffic of people typing you straight into their browser is a strong traffic generator, so, despite it being to your homepage, it is still an easy win.

Social media traffic

Once you have got your organic search traffic game in order, start to focus your efforts, or your marketing team, on a structured approach to social media marketing.

I say structured approach because so many marketers try to be innovative and creative with social media, when it is all about consistency and hard graft with B2B social media posting. Yes, if you are talking to consumers then you can be more creative, but for your target audience and buyer persona, think what they will engage with.

Here is the content mix that engages people on LinkedIn, Twitter and YouTube.

Blog posts

Share your most popular blog posts regularly. On Twitter we share two to three blog posts per day, mixed in with other posts. On LinkedIn I would share blog posts on your company page, then ask your team to re-share them and comment on their personal profiles – commenting is more important.

LinkedIn articles

People focus on posting on LinkedIn, but don't forget the ability to write an article. This will be longer form content and maybe 2,000–3,000 words, but it should be a deep dive into a topic and can include videos, images, quotes and links back to relevant posts on your website.

Go be remarkable: Set up a LinkedIn newsletter. If you activate 'Creator Mode' on your personal LinkedIn profile, you can do a few things such as change your profile picture to a 30-second video. But one of the most powerful things you can do is create a newsletter that will be sent out to all your connections as regularly as you can do it. I recommend one per month. The power of this is that LinkedIn emails everyone for you and lets them know you have posted a new newsletter. You can embed videos, images and links back to your website in these newsletters, so make them interesting and interactive to engage people.

Videos

Sharing video content that is useful and engaging is a great generator of traffic from social media, especially if you include a link back to something relevant in the post or description on YouTube. Remember that videos on Twitter can only be a maximum of 2 minutes 11 seconds.

Keep them short and punchy. Video is also a great way of building out a re-marketing audience from video views, especially on YouTube and LinkedIn.

Live stream

One of the primary sources of traffic I have had in my last three businesses has been from running live events on LinkedIn, Twitter and YouTube. You can run Q&A shows and webinars or just post live from your business and share your company culture – i.e., lift the lid on life in your business.

One of my favourite formats is interviewing people, as it is great content and always attracts good audiences. Think about the people in your industry or target sector who you could invite on to your live show, then use a service such as Streamyard[11] and off you go.

Polls and surveys

People love to engage with polls. They are quick and easy to vote on, so for building out re-marketing audiences and getting people to interact with your feed, they are a winner. A tip here is to do these on your personal feeds rather than the business feeds.

On LinkedIn I have found that polls are engaged with more readily on personal feeds than on a company page. The power of LinkedIn polls is that you can see everyone who has voted on them, then direct message each of those people. So if the poll is relevant to your target audience, then this can be a great way of getting a conversation started.

On Twitter, polls on your company feed will be fine. I also find that promoting polls on Twitter produces a lot of engagement for a small budget. Again, if you are building a re-marketing audience, then this can be gold.

Infographics and images

If you can simplify complex ideas and turn them into an info-graphic, an animated GIF or an image, then this will drive engagement and keep you front of mind. I like to use quotes, testimonials and graphics to tell stories. The visual nature attracts people and stops them scrolling past your message.

---

[11] www.streamyard.com

Use www.canva.com to get started, as they have some incredible design templates you can use.

Testimonials and quotes

I see these being overdone by businesses and, again, it is a bit like 'Look how great we are!' These are very bottom-of-the-funnel pieces of content, so if they hit the 5% of people who are ready to buy, then great. But the other 95% are getting little value from them, so keep them to two or three per week on Twitter and once a week on LinkedIn if you are doing them as a quote graphic.

What does work well, though, is getting your testimonials as short one-minute video testimonials. They are more natural and genuine, especially if not over-produced, and they serve the double purpose of being another piece of video content to build a re-marketing audience from.

Don't forget to become a groupie

The community side of LinkedIn is overlooked by many B2B companies, but there are industry groups for nearly every sector you can imagine – in many cases, there are multiple groups. A simple search for manufacturing groups gives over 16,000 results, and you can see the UK manufacturing groups with 54k and 40k members.

Joining these groups then being an active member can give you excellent penetration into any industry sector and enable you to build a network of contacts quickly.

A word of warning: do not join a group to sell, otherwise you will be banned. Join the group to add value, answer questions and engage. Remember, we are turning a one-to-many conversation into a one-to-one conversation on social media.

> **Go be remarkable:** Get your #hashtag game in order.
> Using hashtags in your post is a great way of getting
> other people to see your content and posts, especially
> industry hashtags. In B2B I try to avoid the 'trending'
> hashtags unless they are relevant to a post. Use services
> such as www.all-hashtag.com to research the most
> relevant industry hashtags to use.

To tag or not to tag, that is the question

This is a bit of a hot topic, as just because you can tag people
into a post does not mean you should do it all the time.

Yes, if your post is super-relevant to people or of interest
to them, then definitely tag them into it, but avoid tagging
people into a post that has nothing to do with them; it can
become tiresome and a little spammy.

Posting frequency is very platform specific

The final point I want to mention is to get your posting
frequency right on each platform.

LinkedIn

Don't overdo it. Post a maximum of twice a day, maybe once
on your personal profile and once on the company page, then
write an article once a week.

Twitter

Post 10–15 times per day. To really break though the noise,
you need to post regularly, almost hourly, as the way people
consume Twitter content is very different. They rarely visit

your profile but simply swipe through Tweets on their feed, hence the lifecycle of a Tweet is around an hour. So post regularly and mix up what you post about using the list above.

YouTube

This is trickier, as I always posted one video per week until Google/YouTube changed the algorithm. Now it appears you need to post daily to stand any chance of getting ranked unless you pay to boost a video. A B2B business should focus on good quality video content, then embed their videos in blog posts, too. This will rank the video and the post in search results more effectively.

Now the organic traffic is really flowing, let's finish by looking at paid traffic generation from ads and re-marketing.

Paid traffic

Over the years, this is an area of marketing that people seem wary of in the B2B sector, usually because they have been burnt in the past by a PPC agency charging too much and delivering very little in terms of tangible leads and revenue.

However, when used in the right way, paid can give you a very scalable source of traffic that returns a healthy positive ROI when optimised correctly. My advice is to identify a good agency that knows what it is doing or even send your marketing executive on intensive paid ads training. This is a source of traffic that you can turn on or off as required – the true definition of a lead generation machine.

The three areas to focus on with paid traffic are:

- **Paid Search** – Google Ads are the way to go and, over the years, they have become far more user friendly.

Google has made the ad platform a far more accessible place for businesses to generate traffic at scale, with better communication from their own team of advisors.

- **Social Paid Ads** – As B2B owners, I recommend you take a long hard look at LinkedIn Campaigns and get the LinkedIn Tag added to your website. The ability to target sectors, roles, size of company and geographical locations makes it a great way to only get in front of the eyeballs you want to be in front of and no one else.

- **Re-Marketing** – The ability to build out custom audiences of people who have visited your website, even specific pages on your website, and engaged with your social content, such as watching videos, voting in polls and commenting on posts, has opened up a world of personalised ads that was unheard of a decade ago. When you get your head around this, it will be a game changer for you.

The way I recommend you approach your paid campaigns is to give a quick boost to the organic traffic you are generating. Let's look in more detail at each and how to approach them.

Paid search

If you have built out a reasonable keyword list, then you will be able to identify the 'intent' keywords and phrases in your list. These are the words people use when making buying decisions or in the consideration stage of their buying journey, so they will not be short, broad phrases but longer-tail phrases of three to five words. If you build out Ad Sets in Google Ads around these words, then you will have a great start to your first campaign.

Google Ads can also run on YouTube and allows you to set up custom audiences to re-market to people who watch your videos or other videos on topics that you feel your target audience would consume.

Make sure you add the Google pixel to your website so that you can build out re-marketing audiences of people who visit it. Your campaigns can then be split between generating fresh search traffic and re-marketing to people who are already aware of your brand and have expressed an interest by visiting your website.

As I touched on at the start of this chapter, make sure all your paid ads are directing the traffic to a landing page that is relevant to the ad they have just responded to, a page that has been tested and optimised for conversions. I still see people running paid campaigns to their homepage that don't convert, so they don't think paid traffic works.

I have worked with companies who have used paid ads, worked hard to optimise them and gone from losing money to breaking even and then making £5 for every £1 they spend on them.

It is an iterative process of optimisation, and once you get to the stage of a profitable campaign, it is just a matter of increasing your budget to increase your lead flow, so don't give up. Make sure you keep optimising to reach this point – it's worth it.

Social media paid ads

I am going to address the elephant in the room here – LinkedIn Ads are expensive. But when used correctly, they are incredibly effective at getting the right target person engaging with your business.

The secret is not to sell. When you use LinkedIn ads, try to add value and start a conversation with your Primary Buyer Persona, then the ads become more reasonable and are far more successful.

Make sure your ad targeting and filters are dialled in so the only people who see them are your target audience, then offer value, by which I mean offer:

- A free report
- A free webinar
- A free diagnostic tool or scorecard

All three work well and add value. I have personally used all three and the report is still the best to get started with, especially if you work hard to make it remarkable! Don't just produce a piece of generic content that is little more than a blog post in PDF form; put some deep work into writing your free report and make sure it addresses pain points, shares valuable insights and is something that makes people feel you have given real value to them.

The power of social media lead generation from paid ads is that all people need to do is click a button to say they are interested and their details will be pre-populated in the form, so it is an easy, frictionless way of building lists.

The additional bonus is that many modern CRMs such as HubSpot have a direct integration with paid ads, both Google and LinkedIn, so you can accurately measure the volume of leads and ROI you are seeing from your ads.

Re-marketing ads

I hope you picked up my excitement about this type of paid ad earlier but if not, let me say this: if you do no other paid advertising at all, make sure you become an expert on using re-marketing pixels and building out custom audiences. In my experience this is the best place to start investing your money, as the audience is generally warm and aware of you already so converts at a higher rate than a cold audience.

Set up your Google Ads account and LinkedIn Campaign Manager, then put the re-marketing tag/pixel on your website, normally in the header, so that it tracks all pages.

Next, set up the type of audience. I would start with 'Website Visitors', which builds a master audience list of everyone who visits your website. Then one of my favourites is 'Video Views' and finally a 'Post Engagement' audience to capture people who comment, like, share and engage with your posts on LinkedIn. Remember that polls are some of the most engaged-with posts on the platform, so this is one reason I recommend you use them regularly in your content mix.

The conversion paradox

Whenever I meet with clients and we start discussing ways to grow their business, I will inevitably hear: 'Well, if we only had more leads, the business would grow', then, as we dig into this, I see all the effort they are putting into their lead generation, spending money on paid ads, on SEO services, creating more and more content, producing videos and trying to create more traffic.

But the sad thing is that 90% of businesses have more than enough traffic, and when I look at their email lists and database, they have more than enough leads. The real problem is conversion; they simply have not conversion optimised their website to convert visitors into leads or the stages of their sales process to convert leads into customers and revenue.

I equate this to pouring water into a leaky bucket: you can continue pouring water into the bucket, but it will keep leaking. As a business you can continue to drive traffic and leads into a funnel, but you are wasting money if you have not optimised every step to convert.

So I want to finish this chapter on traffic by telling you to focus on conversion first, then see how much more traffic you actually need to generate.

But more on that in the next chapter, when we go deep on engagement and how to effectively engage with your audience at different stages of the journey.

Summary

I hope this chapter has put to rest any fears you had about generating traffic. In my experience, the challenge lies not in generating the traffic but in converting that traffic into leads and those leads into customers.

Exercise #7 – Keyword research and setting up your content creation

Head over to www.goberemarkable.com/resources and download the Keyword Content Tracker.

This is a spreadsheet that will allow you to track 12 keywords for each of four topics in the tabs at the bottom.

You should end up with a list of around 48 of your top keyword phrases that you need to rank for in Google and other search engines. This can also be used to plan out your blog posts, videos and pillar pages on your website, so is a great content tracker.

8. STEPS: Principle 3 – Engagement

Remarkable engagement converts into natural sales conversations

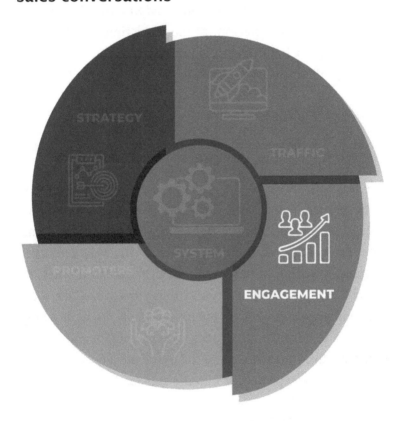

By principle 3 of the STEPS Growth Method, you will have created multiple sources of traffic coming into your business, with a focus on attracting highly targeted website traffic. The next stage is to build out how you engage with this traffic to initially convert it into leads in your CRM, then how you nurture those leads into natural sales conversations and move them along your optimised sales process to becoming a customer.

In your growth strategy, you should have identified areas to process out in your sales plan, marketing plan and service and support strategy that require engagement.

Great engagement is built on providing the right information to the right person, at the right time, in the right format and in a highly personalised manner.

We achieve this in five ways.

Create engaging content

We looked at the power of educational and insightful content when we discussed developing your website blog, but alongside this content we need conversion content such as guides, white papers, videos and checklists that will connect and engage the audience in the right way. If you are developing your keywords and content tracker in the way I recommended, you should have a wealth of topics to discuss, so create a range of content around these topics and see what your audience engages with the most – i.e., if you write a blog post on a topic and your visitors love the content and read it, then turn this into a video and the topic into a downloadable guide where you go deeper into the subject.

Develop your conversational strategy

You must understand how your persona likes to communicate, then develop these channels of communication to remove any friction. Do they like to telephone, email, engage through social media, messenger, use chat bots or live chat? Or are they still more comfortable with face to face? Either way I recommend making the three most popular conversational channels your priority and asking people constantly how they prefer to engage with you.

Understand where they are in their buying journey

This will allow you to keep the conversations relevant and provide them with the right information to keep them moving forward. As we have already discussed, the type of content they are consuming will be a strong indicator as to where they are in their journey.

Define the next steps in the journey

We have discussed having a structured sales process, and this allows you or your sales team to keep the momentum going and control the process while always looking for the win-win for all sides. The more transparent you can be as you engage across the sales process, the better.

Client engagement post-sale

We will look at this in more detail in the next chapter, but this will be one of the areas that sets you apart from 90% of your competition and gives you the competitive advantage. In this chapter, I will go deeper into the 'how' of great engagement and share what I have seen working over the last decade so that you get it right from day one.

Turn your website into a hub of valuable content and insights

The starting point is to re-imagine your website and turn it into a resource and community hub for your primary buyer and target market to visit and use. As I have discussed earlier in this book, the B2B sector is particularly bad at this and tends to have a website that is little more than an online brochure about them.

The modern website, though, is used to initially connect and engage your audience before converting them into a lead, so you must have a number of ways of delivering valuable content that is irresistible to your visitors. These include:

Blogs

Create a blog full of valuable solution content that covers all stages of the journey – i.e., top-of-the-funnel content that helps the visitor understand and define their problems, middle-of-the-funnel content that allows them to refine and understand the options for solving the problem and bottom-of-the-funnel content to allow them to make a decision that is right for them.

> **Go be remarkable:** Use guest bloggers to create content. A strategy I have used many times is to identify and approach guest bloggers to write a couple of blog posts per month in return for a name check and link back to their website. I would always check the piece they have written, but, again, it adds variety to your blog and the guest will also promote it to their audience, so, if you can find a micro-influencer with a highly targeted audience that fits yours, you will gain additional visitors to your own website.

Gated and ungated resources

Include a resources section full of videos, reports, checklists and guides that will help the visitor, some gated that they need to exchange their contact details for and some ungated or totally free. By constantly adding to your resources and helping buyers answer questions and make the right decisions, you will be engaging in a human, helpful way.

A big mistake I see many businesses making here is to gate everything. In the early days of a relationship, you want to nurture trust and build authority. Once you have that, people will happily share their details with you, so take it slowly. Don't propose marriage on the first date.

Chat bots and live chat

Everyone I speak to has a personal view about using chat bots and live chat on their website, and the negative responses are usually from people who have been on a website where the chat bot has not been set up correctly and is not fit for purpose.

However, if you take the time to set up your chat bots and live chat correctly, you will see them converting better than any other channel. I recommend that you initially use them to answer FAQs and queries. These can be automated or live chat. I have used the free HubSpot Chatbot on multiple websites and it is incredibly powerful, especially when driven by the page they are on. For example, we put one on our pricing page that said: 'We can see you are looking at our pricing. Is there anything we can help you find?' – so it was very relevant and we knew that the people who were on this page were bottom of the funnel and near a decision.

Remember to keep all of this very visible; don't bury it away. On your homepage, have sections that link to your blog posts and resources, with the same in your navigation, so you encourage people to connect with you and they can easily find useful content when they arrive on your website.

Optimise your website for conversions

As a follow-on from your activity with the use of content on your website, it is critical to optimise for conversions and send your visitors down predictable conversion paths across your site.

An example of a simple conversion path would be:

- **Call To Action** – A button, link or banner-style CTA.
- **Landing Page** – When clicked on, the CTA leads to a landing page that has a relevant offer and form to complete.
- **Thank You Page** – If the visitor completes the form and submits their details, they are taken to a thank you page for the delivery of the offer.

This is a simple example, but it allows a conversion metric to be taken at each stage of the process – i.e., how many people clicked on the CTA, how many people visited the landing page, how many people completed the form and how many went to the thank you page and downloaded the offer.

By measuring these data points, you can split test, optimise and improve your conversion without the need for increasing your traffic. You will develop multiple conversion paths across your website that traffic can go down and this will enable you to hit the 2% conversion goal we set, increasing it to 5% and more with optimisation.

Developing remarkable conversion content and offers

The secret to website conversion is having valuable pieces of content that add value to the visitor's journey, are educational and answer their questions. So, again, it goes back to understanding your buyer's journey and the problems, questions, mistakes and payoffs they are looking for answers to as they move along their journey towards making a decision. Focus on creating a valuable content offer that contains insights into these.

The six most successful content offers I have used with clients are:

- Reports
- Guides
- Self-diagnostic tools such as a scorecard
- Checklists
- Video series
- Webinars/live shows

Each of these can be used to deliver the right information at the right time. A guide could be informative and educational to suit the awareness stage of the buying journey, but then, as they need to know more specific information and move into the consideration and decision stages, checklists or webinars become super important to deliver more detail.

Go be remarkable: Optimise your blog posts for conversion. When you have put effort into writing valuable blog posts and sharing them regularly to drive traffic to them, you must have calls to action in multiple places in them. I would have a link in the first paragraph, a banner halfway through and a banner at the end of the post. At my agency Digital Media Edge, 48% of our leads came from people clicking on a call to action in a blog post.

Use your chat bots for conversion

As discussed above, something I recommend you take seriously on your website is setting up a chat bot that is available to answer questions and trigger engagement 24 hours a day.

I agree that when not set up correctly they serve little purpose, but spend time thinking through what questions people ask regularly on specific pages on your website and set up a bot specifically for that page to answer them; plus, use your bots to deliver content offers or links to landing pages and you have an automated conversion tool that is built around engagement.

Imagine you use it on your services page and you set up different branch logic, so if someone answers questions in a certain way, they go down one route, and if they answer in other ways, they are taken down a different route, all the time sharing useful information and providing data about themselves, data that is added directly to their contact record in your CRM.

A great example of using chat bots in the right way and something to model yours on is the way Gong uses it;[12] it is engaging, humorous and useful.

In fact, their entire website is worth digging into to see how a modern B2B website should be structured.

So learn the lessons, set them up correctly and your chat bots and live chat can become your engagement secret weapon.

Engage on social media in the right way

One area that people seem to get repeatedly wrong is the way in which they use social media, and particularly LinkedIn, to connect and engage with people. There is little more frustrating than receiving a connection request and connecting with someone, only to get a clearly automated response or a long sales message back.

The key with social media is to be social, so by all means spend your time reaching out to relevant people, but then engage with them first before sending a connection request. My advice on this is to:

- Do your research – Spend time looking through their profile; look for common ground or something they have achieved so you are relevant when you do reach out to connect. I also look at their job title and work out what they are responsible for and how they may see success.
- Visit their website and do some background research on their company. Again, I look for any awards they

---

[12] www.gong.io

have won or milestones they have achieved so I can be relevant.

- One thing I find opens conversations up is if the business is clearly recruiting, as this means they are growing. So I will often help them by sharing any job adverts with my network.
- Engage with them – Look at their posts, like, comment and share a post if possible so they notice you being engaging.
- Now reach out and connect; always put a short note with your connection request mentioning any things you have uncovered in your research.
- Once you are connected, thank them for connecting and ask how things are going
- I recommend being conversational for a few days and, again, engaging with their posts, then sharing something useful – a blog post, a video, a report – or you could invite them to a webinar, whatever you think will be helpful and useful to them.

Your goal here is to connect, engage, educate and develop the relationship before adding them to your CRM and emailing them.

I always think that, to be remarkable on social media, you need to be good at listening and find the opportunity to turn what is a one-to-many platform into a one-to-one conversation.

Regular emails are at the heart of your lead nurture

Email is still one of the most effective forms of marketing and lead nurturing, with a recent survey by the Data Marketing

Association[13] revealing that the average ROI on email marketing now stands at £42 for every £1 spent.

So make sure you develop robust email marketing campaigns, including:

- **Lead generation** – Straight-up email marketing, by emailing your growing lists of contacts with valuable content and sharing free webinars and videos.

- **Lead nurture** – Every offer download that has converted a visitor into a lead needs to have an automated sequence of emails crafted to follow up. I recommend a follow-up campaign of five to eight emails, each aimed at building your relationship and setting up a meeting.

- **Re-engagement** – A slower drip of emails out to colder contacts in your list who are not engaged or in a buying cycle. I recommend you use re-engagement campaigns to activate or delete a contact, unless they are in a Target Account that you want to nurture over a longer period of time.

  You do not want to build large lists of unengaged contacts, as this will damage your email open rates and could impact on deliverability, whereas a list of highly engaged contacts who open emails and click on the links will boost your deliverability, so don't go for volume. I would prefer a small list of 4,000 people who are highly engaged to a large list of 40,000 who never open or engage.

- **Client engagement** – Finally, don't forget to set up a process for regular emails and engagement with your

---

[13] www.dma.org.uk

customers. Invite them to events, share content that is only for customers, develop a newsletter to keep them up to date with developments in the business and new products and show them how much you appreciate them being a customer.

Go be remarkable: Use video in your emails. One of the most engaging forms of media is video and, with services such as www.vidyard.com enabling the embedding of videos direct into Outlook or Gmail, or even into social media messages, this can allow very personalised outreach, especially by the sales team. I have used this approach over the past three years with huge success: my open rates increased by 30% and the engagement and feedback I got was great. My approach would be to do some research on a prospect or lead, then visit their website and record a live video of me looking through their site, offering some tips for improvement, so leading with value. I would always mention them by name at the start and then embed the video, including an animated thumbnail, into the email, with a link to my calendar for them to plan a meeting to discuss my thoughts. This was one of the highest converting approaches I have ever used.

Optimising your sales engagement

The final critical part of engagement is your sales. The modern approach to selling is very consultative, as you can see in the inbound sales methodology graphic. We align our stages of the sales process – Identify, Connect, Explore and Advise – with the buyer's journey stages – Awareness, Consideration and Decision – so it is a natural progression. The goal is to avoid selling to them but to help them make the right decision, and to put ourselves in the best position to be the one they choose at the end of the process.

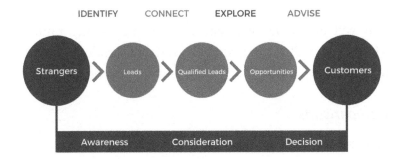

Inbound Sales Methodology

In his book *They Ask, You Answer*, Marcus Sheridan describes content as the greatest sales tool in the world today. As you think about your business and sales process, you can see the importance of developing engaging content that addresses questions as prospects move along their buying journey.[14]

Think about how you can produce engaging content around the following:

Qualification

A great way to use engaging content is to pre-qualify people by their level of interest and genuine intent. A good example of this was the way we used content at Digital Media Edge.

---

[14] M. Sheridan, *They Ask, You Answer* (2017).

Following a connect call, we would send out a recap of the call, along with a questionnaire to be completed and a video of how we worked to be watched prior to the next exploratory call. Our statistics showed that those people who completed the questionnaire and watched the video were 65% more likely to go on and become a customer, and those who did not were unlikely to go any further.

Pricing

This will be the number one question in people's minds: 'How much will it cost?', so make sure you produce content to answer this and be transparent on your pricing page.

Comparisons

The chances are high that you will not be the only solution your buyer is considering to address their problem, so be ready to embrace the different options and competitors they may be considering and use content to address this – it is a reality.

Problems

It is natural for people to focus their mind on the negatives, and if you look at the searches on Google, far more are negative than positive – i.e., 'The problems with…'. With this in mind, address any problems that you feel the buyer needs to be aware of; again, putting their mind at rest here rather than hoping it does not come up in conversation is a big win. The trust you will gain by being open and transparent will always strengthen the relationship.

Objections

Talk to your sales team and uncover the most common objection they hear from people who do not go ahead. Now prepare content to engage about this earlier in the process so it is openly discussed and resolved. An objection is just another form of question that has not been answered.

The more helpful and engaging you can make your sales process, the higher it will convert for you and the more predictably your business will grow.

Summary – Be human, holistic and helpful

Engagement is process driven, and mapping out the areas that will impact lead generation, customer acquisition and client engagement is key to building a remarkable engagement process.

I hope that, by sharing what I have seen working well over the past decade, you will be able to build out your processes and unlock natural conversations with your prospects and clients. As discussed above, focus on:

- turning your website into a hub of valuable content, insights and resources
- optimising your website for conversions and engagement
- engaging across social media in the right way
- using email to nurture and engage to build relationships
- creating an engaging sales process.

If you take action in these areas and follow the advice I have shared, you will connect and engage with the visitors to your business in the right way, being human, holistic and helpful.

Exercise #8 – Complete your content creation grid

Visit www.goberemarkable.com/resources and download a blank content creation grid, with the types of content you can create on the left and the stages of the buying journey you are impacting with the content. Engagement is all about the right content being delivered at the right time to the right person.

Spend time with your team on completing this grid by filling in the title of the piece of content in each square, what question it is answering and what format it will take – i.e., produce a guide on increasing efficiency for manufacturing businesses.

9. STEPS: Principle 4 – Promoters

Delighted customers will naturally turn into promoters of your business and are one of the most valuable assets you have

Over the past 30 years, every remarkable business I have come across, been a customer of or helped build has had an almost fanatical obsession with client engagement. They appreciate all the investment that has gone into creating the customer relationship and they focus on making the customer feel valued; they want the customer experience to be remarkable.

So the final process you must have in place is for iterative client engagement that I call 'the promoters process'. This will make sure that you maximise the value that your customer base offers your business for raising awareness, generating new leads and growing your revenue.

When you have remarkable delivery of your core product, service or solution, you will produce delighted customers who rave about the experience they have had with you. These advocates will do a lot of the heavy lifting for you, by actively promoting your business to everyone they know and speak to.

My advice is to not leave this to chance but to have processes in place to ensure this happens the same way every time. So in this phase of STEPS, we will focus on building out processes for the following seven areas:

- Consistent client engagement
- Regular sending of customer surveys
- Development of products exclusively for customers
- Generation of reviews
- Creation of case studies
- A pipeline of testimonials
- Requesting of referrals

Engage regularly with your clients and customers

It sounds obvious, but I can assure you that the majority of businesses I speak to do not do this well, if they do it at all. They spend all that money and effort generating new leads and customers, but the biggest opportunity they actually have in their business is sitting in their existing customer base.

I spent some time working with a large law firm that had several branches across the UK. They had a client base of 64,000 clients that they had done work for over the past 40 years and when I started working with them, they emailed this list once a year at Christmas.

Our focus in the first three months was on a re-engagement campaign to their client base, setting up a newsletter to share stories and useful information but also to ensure that every client knew of the range of services on offer across all the departments of the practice. The core work they did was commercial, but they also dealt with family law, wills and probate and conveyancing, and they had a large litigation department for personal injury and negligence work.

We emailed the client base weekly and also set up a live event to which we invited people to show we appreciated their business. This campaign generated £680k in new instructions and fees over the initial six-month period.

So ensure you set up a process for regular client engagement; identify the best mix of emails, newsletters, events, calls and gifts that show you appreciate them and value their custom.

Go be remarkable: Call your customers personally. I want you, as the owner of the business, to make it one of your highest priority tasks to pick five customers each month, at random, and call them to speak to them. This will set you apart from 99% of other companies and make you remarkable, plus you will learn so much in these calls.

Survey your customers to constantly improve and evolve what you do

I want you to be honest here: when was the last time you sent a survey out to your customers for any type of feedback? Surveys are not just about finding out how satisfied people are; they improve your depth of understanding, and the constant feedback of information will ensure you constantly innovate and evolve what you do.

There are three types of survey I recommend you focus on:

- Satisfaction survey
- Persona survey
- Jobs-to-be-done survey

The way to get these surveys completed is not to send them once then forget about them but to have regular survey emails that go out to clients, using your CRM to segment the audience into those who have completed each survey type and those who have not. We will look at all three shortly.

In HubSpot I use active lists to do this so that when someone completes a survey, they are moved into a 'completed' list. This prevents me from annoying clients who have already completed a survey.

Use Survey Monkey to automate your surveys

The best tool I have used for all three types is Survey Monkey.[15] Best of all, the free version allows you to get started with a ten-question survey. However, I would upgrade to the

---

[15] www.surveymonkey.com

£32-per-month plan, which allows unlimited surveys and unlimited questions per survey, plus up to 15,000 responses per year – more than enough for most businesses.

Go be remarkable: Integrate Survey Monkey into your CRM. The most powerful feature of Survey Monkey is the ability to integrate it into your CRM and other tools. HubSpot has a built-in integration and allows a two-way sync of data between the two pieces of software, so you can send surveys in emails, automate workflows to send them out and take the responses back into your contact records, using the information to trigger other actions or tasks.

Creating a satisfaction survey

The starting point for your customer surveys should always be around your core offering and how satisfied the customer is with their buying journey and the product, service or solution you have provided, any improvements they can recommend and how likely they are to recommend you to their friends or colleagues.

The aim is to obtain valuable feedback that you can take action on, not just to pat yourself on the back for what a great job you are doing. Constant innovation and improvement are our goals when building a remarkable business, as with this mindset you will create a true competitive advantage in your marketplace and your competition will never threaten you.

So focus your questions on:

Core service, product or solution usage

You need to understand what people like, what people don't like and what you can improve. This is vital for customer retention and reducing customer churn.

Satisfaction scale

How satisfied were they with your service and working with you as a customer? Give them a scale of 1 to 10 in key areas of your business, such as buying experience, likelihood to recommend, likelihood to purchase again, website usability and service and support received. Your Net Promoter Score (NPS) comes from this section.

Longevity

Finally, include some questions about the on-going relationship, such as follow-up contact permission, product improvement, upgrades and onboarding resources.

Setting up a buyer persona survey

We discussed the importance of understanding exactly who our buyer is, their sources of information, the challenges they are trying to solve, the mistakes they are making, the solutions they look at and why they make buying decisions.

I believe this is an ongoing process so that we understand the buyer better than they understand themselves. Therefore, in order to mature your Primary Buyer Personas, creating a separate survey that just focuses on this is powerful. Yes, we could include it in the customer satisfaction survey, but then you are adding another 10–15 questions that will reduce the chances of a customer completing it.

So in our buyer persona survey or interview, we focus on:

- **Demographics** – Who they are, i.e., age, location, gender, marital status, number of children, education, level of income, job title, industry.
- **Psychographics** – Why they do what they do. Uncover habits and tendencies, as these will often determine why they buy. These questions will be around sources of information, their shopping habits, the technology they use, their priorities, their roadblocks, their challenges, their favourite social media platforms, their likes and dislikes, etc.

I recommend that, every six months, you pick out 15 customers who fit your ideal customer profile and buyer persona. Invite them to complete a structured persona interview with you, where you ask them 25–30 key questions.

Remember: this information is invaluable to your understanding of who you are talking to, what a good fit lead looks like, the challenges they are trying to solve and how you can help them.

Using a jobs-to-be-done survey

Once you have a well-defined buyer persona in place, you will know the type of person who is most likely to use your product, service or solution. The next step is to understand what would cause them to buy from you. We make buying decisions based on what we are trying to get done, a result or an outcome, not on the things happening to us. So the better you can understand what 'job' your customers were trying to get done when they used you, the more of those people you can focus on attracting and the better understanding you will have of their buying journey.

Again, this can be done through a survey or through interviewing your existing customers. The goal is to understand what was important to them at each stage of the buying process, building out a timeline and pattern of events on why and how they became a customer. We can also measure how long this timeline was.

So we start at the end and move backwards along this path of events when asking:

- Why did you buy the product, solution or service?
- How long did you think about it before making the decision?
- What was it that made you go through with the sale?
- Had you thought about buying before but not done it?
- Were you making do with something else (or nothing at all)?
- When did you realise that you did not have to 'make do' anymore?
- What was the series of events from realisation to becoming a customer?

As with your persona survey, map this out with 15 customers, then try to come up with a story that covers everyone's answers. This will give you a jobs-to-be-done story as follows:

'As a {WHO} when I am {SITUATION} I want to {MOTIVATION} so that I can {OUTCOME}.'

A great example of this is when McDonald's interviewed customers about their purchase of milkshakes through the day. By following this process, they discovered that commuters were purchasing early in the morning for the trip to work. The jobs-to-be-done story was along these lines: 'As a morning commuter, when I am driving to work, I want to eat a snack so that I can keep myself occupied during my commute and get through the first few hours of work without having to stop for a snack.' By knowing this, McDonald's could make sure the milkshakes were thicker in the morning. In contrast, their survey also threw up the fact that, at weekends and in the evenings, the customers for milkshakes were predominantly fathers with their children, so they did not want a thick milkshake that took their child an hour to drink. McDonald's was able to respond to this data by making the milkshakes thinner in the evening and at weekends.

I hope you can see the power of these three surveys in how you constantly innovate and develop your business with a buyer-centric focus.

Create a range of products for your customers

Happy customers are the people who will come back and buy from you repeatedly. Once they have used your core offer and love it, they will naturally want to know what else you do and what's next. In his book *Purple Cow*, Seth Godin writes: 'Do you have the email addresses of the 20 percent of your customer base that loves what you do? If not, start getting them. If you do, what could you make for these customers that would be super-special?' This sums up your approach to creating new products for your customers.[16]

---

[16] S. Godin, *Purple Cow: Transform Your Business by Being Remarkable* (2005).

In some sectors or with some products, they will come back to buy your core product over and over, but with the majority of B2B businesses, there are other products that can be offered, even partnerships with other businesses who offer a complementary service or product, so this is usually high-profit for your business.

A great example of this is the car industry and how they maximise customer brand loyalty. I drive a Mercedes, but alongside the vehicle there are multiple additional services, such as Mercedes Finance, which I used to buy the car. Servicing is offered at the local Mercedes dealership, which I use and pay more for, even though I know a local reputable garage could do exactly the same job. I buy Mercedes-approved parts because I perceive they are better quality, when I know in reality that there are many alternatives that would be cheaper and do the job just as well. I think the only time I really shop around for anything is when it comes to tyres.

So what should a product for clients look like? The most successful ones are premium products – these should be high value to the client and high profit for the business.

As I talked about above, this can be a complementary product, service or solution from another business that you promote in return for a good commission or referral fee. In your quest to grow to £1m turnover, adding easy hands-off revenue like this can often be preferable to adding in another resource intensive product that you need to provide. So think through how you develop these additional revenue streams into the business.

Ask every happy customer to leave a review

The power of other people talking about you, rather than you talking about yourself, is the most valuable content that can be created.

We all use reviews to make buying decisions, and as your buyer moves into the decision-making stage of their journey, they will be looking to decide on who to use from a shortlist of vendors.

I can guarantee that they will search for reviews and opinions from other people who have been customers of yours and used your service or product, such as:

- Google reviews
- LinkedIn recommendations
- Facebook reviews
- Reviews on Trustpilot, Feefo and other third-party review platforms
- Forum reviews – Yes, they will see people discussing you actively on forums and chat. This can be overlooked by many businesses, so set up monitoring of mentions to make sure you are alerted to this.

When someone becomes a customer, ensure you set up a process for asking them to leave a review about their experience with you. Maybe set this to go out three months after they have started using your product, service or solution. The most powerful reviews are those from people who have been with you for a period of time.

Make your clients the stars by producing case studies on their success

What is your case study process? Again, it should be part of your marketing team's role to produce a case study each month.

In simple terms, a case study shows three things:

- a specific challenge that a business has faced
- the solution that solved the challenge
- the results that the business experienced once it had solved the challenge.

Keep your case studies simple, short and easy to consume so that they can be shared with prospective new customers, especially if they are relevant to their industry.

> **Go be remarkable:** Remarkable case studies win awards. You will be expected to provide evidence and examples of the work you do and the results you have achieved if you start applying for awards and recognition, so make this a priority and do it well.

I would recommend that you use a blog post format to produce your case studies, then develop a case study category. I prefer this approach because you can easily link to these case studies: they can be included in your navigation, appear on your blog page, be shared socially and they will also rank well for SEO.

Remember: you are telling the story of a successful relationship you have had with a client, so focus on making the client the star and sharing their success as a result of working with you.

I found that using a video interview with the client and embedding that into the case study was a powerful way to create impact, but it also gives you two formats to share. We would also upload the video to our YouTube channel, and these were some of the most viewed videos we had on there.

Make sure you share your cases studies every day on social media

As you build your library of case studies, make sure they are featured on your website homepage and get pulled in to key pages such as pricing and services. Above all, publish them to Twitter and LinkedIn and the videos to YouTube. These will attract people who relate to them and see themselves facing the challenges you solved.

I regularly work with clients who have some incredible case study stories to tell, yet they do not shout about them enough. They seem to know how to approach asking a client for a case study or how to produce it, but they are not sharing the stories anywhere near enough on social media.

Remember: you are making your client the star here, so tag them in and share freely. Social proof like this is invaluable in helping people align themselves with you and see you as the natural solution to their challenge.

Use case studies in your sales process

One of the key uses of a case study is to share it with prospective new clients. Again, having these as a video works well: if you find a potential new client with a problem you have already solved in their industry, then you can share the example of how you approached it before and the great results you delivered.

Request testimonials from your customers

Along the same lines as case studies, a customer testimonial is another powerful piece of social proof where a happy client talks about you rather than you talking about yourself.

The key here is to keep them short and pull key snippets of text out, if you are using a written testimonial. Earlier in this chapter we discussed sending satisfaction surveys out to customers, and these can be a great source of positive testimonial quotes.

If you discover a great quote, then contact the customer and ask if you could have a meeting to thank them and record a quick video of them talking about their experience working with you. If they are not comfortable on video, then ask for a written testimonial and a picture of them to show they are a real person. The final option is to offer to write the testimonial for the client and ask them to approve it.

Ask your customers for referrals

The final piece of the client engagement and promoters phase is probably the most valuable to your company, and that is putting in place a process for requesting referrals of people your client knows who would benefit from using you or who have similar challenges to the ones you have just solved for the client.

> **Go be remarkable:** Use LinkedIn to mine for introductions. One approach I have used that worked really well is the LinkedIn referral route, where you look through your happy customers' contacts on LinkedIn

and identify anyone who fits your criteria for a good fit business or person. You then connect with them and ask if your client would do you the favour of introducing you.

The fact that a referral is four times more likely to make a purchase and have a 37% higher retention rate demonstrates the value of developing a referral process in your business.

The way I recommend you do this is as follows:

1. **Email** – Three months after they become your client, once they have used your service, product or solution for a period of time, send them an email to thank them for their custom, then ask if they can think of anyone who would be interested in talking to you.
2. **Call** – Follow up your email with a call to the client and ask a second time.
3. **Email** – Identify a list of contacts on LinkedIn that fit your good fit criteria. Send these across to your client and ask if they would introduce you to these people.

The key here is consistency and to set up a process that everyone uses. Your service and support team are best positioned to do this or your sales and account management teams, who have a strong relationship, can make this a very natural process.

Summary

This final set of processes is all about unlocking the value that your base of existing customers offers you and your business.

If you take the time to get off the hamster wheel of producing a constant stream of new leads for a minute and focus your time on your existing customers, you will unearth a mountain of value and revenue. Remember that the cost of acquisition has already been incurred, so this will be higher-profit revenue too.

Every client I have worked with has multiple opportunities in their customer database, opportunities that will increase revenue with little fresh investment needed, apart from putting in place several processes. So take the time to do the exercises at the end of this chapter and put in place processes for:

- Regular client engagement
- Surveys
- Requesting reviews
- Writing case studies
- Creating video testimonials
- Asking for referrals
- Cross sell and upsell opportunities with additional products for clients

When you get this right, you will be a truly remarkable business that delights customers and maximises every opportunity to grow revenue in the most effective way.

Exercise #9 – Call five customers

I want you to compile a list of five customers who fit your Primary Buyer Persona and make it your job to call each of them in the next week.

You are going to thank them for being a customer and tell them how much you appreciate their business. Then ask if they could answer five questions for you:

1. Are they happy with the service you have provided?
2. Would they recommend you to their friends or colleagues?
3. If there was one thing they could change about your product, what would it be?
4. What was the problem they were trying to solve when they started looking for your product?
5. How did your product help them solve that problem?

Let me know how you get on by emailing me at richard@goberemarkable.com – I would be genuinely interested to hear your story.

10. STEPS: Principle 5 – System

Building a connected single source of truth at the heart of your business

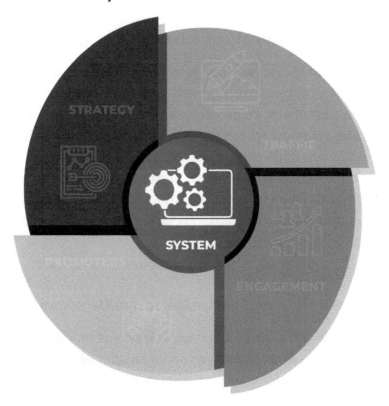

Aremarkable system is connected and easy to use. It will act as a single source of truth and measure everything, allowing you to make those data-driven decisions on exactly what is working, what is not working and what can be improved and optimised. At the heart of your business is your system of tools, technology and software, which, when set up correctly, will enable you to grow at scale.

In this chapter I will look at how to put that system together, the key elements you need in a modern business system and how to use a platform such as HubSpot to build a core growth system that can drive scalable growth.

The eight elements of a remarkable system

At the end of Chapter 4, your exercise was to audit your current technology stack of software, apps and tools and make a list of how many were connected, how many talked to each other and where you were duplicating functionality. I asked you to do this because, in 99% of the businesses I visit, the technology has grown organically and been driven by individual people with a favourite tool or something they want to use rather than the tools that are going to support the business most effectively.

The eight elements you need in your core system are:

Customer relationship management (CRM) software

CRM software is for storing every contact and touchpoint. It must allow easy segmentation and list building of contacts in order to personalise communications and keep them relevant.

Website

Your website is part of your system and needs to be connected. You need to know who is visiting your website and what they are reading, and you need to be able to convert those visitors into leads in your CRM. You also need a fast, secure and mobile-optimised site that has a great user experience.

Administration and communication tools

Tools such as email, calendars, spreadsheets, word processor, PowerPoint, Messenger, Zoom/Teams, telephone and chat bots/live chat.

Marketing tools

Marketing tools for effective traffic and lead generation, including landing pages, forms, calls to action, blogs, chat bots, email automation, social media management, lead scoring, marketing automation and marketing analytics and reporting.

Sales tools

You will need sales tools, including sales pipeline, email sequences, meetings, video, task creation, quoting and sales analytics and reporting.

Operational delivery

This may be an ERP, WMS or other software for your specific product, service or solution delivery. My advice here is to make sure it is a modern cloud-based system.

Service and support tools

These will include a ticketing system for support queries, ticket automation, live chat, Messenger and a knowledgebase for FAQs.

Finance tools

Modern cloud-based accounting software from Xero, Sage or QuickBooks will integrate easily with your system.

I am sure there are many other pieces of software that would be 'nice to have', but these eight will give you the foundations of a solid core system that will help you to grow at scale and give your team the tools to succeed, so let's look in more detail at each.

Your CRM is your single source of truth

I cannot understand any business that is still relying on using Excel spreadsheets and out-of-date databases when there are so many great pieces of CRM software on the market that cost very little to set up and implement.

I hope you took my advice in Chapter 4 and spent some time researching and identifying a piece of CRM software that fits your needs. In B2B business, where we are selling to other businesses and particular people within those businesses, it is critical to get this right, as there will be multiple touchpoints and people involved in a decision-making process, especially where it is a considered purchase that takes place over a number of months or years.

> **Go be remarkable:** As a business owner you must make sure that all this information is stored centrally. I hear time and time again about businesses that have lost a salesperson who took all the information and contacts with them. This is commercially damaging and so easily prevented by adopting a CRM.

So what are you looking for in a good CRM? Above all it must be easy to use and intuitive, and it must be used by everyone across the business. As soon as you get something that is complicated and takes up too much time, you will find that people stop using it. In my businesses we had this a number of times, where some people liked a system and others hated it, so the data was never up to date. I only found that this changed when we moved to HubSpot, and I have used this platform in my last three businesses. It is a pleasure to use, easy to keep up to date and extremely powerful. The core elements of your CRM are built around:

- **Contacts** – Individual records of people, their details and any engagement with those people.
- **Companies** – Company records will show the firmographic details of a business and the contact(s) within that business.
- **Target accounts** – If you operate a B2B business, then being able to target high-value accounts you work with or want to work with is powerful, especially if you are using an account-based marketing approach.
- **Lists** – The ability to segment your contacts into relevant lists based on activity is key to keeping your engagement relevant and timely. You will need customer lists, prospect lists, event attendee lists, lists for people coming from different lead sources – all are important, especially if you use list membership as a trigger for marketing and email automation.
- **Deals** – A good CRM will allow you to set up and track deals at a contact and company level.
- **Activity** – Your CRM needs to track all activity at a contact and company level, including emails

exchanged, calls made, notes on meetings, engagement with your website, deals set up, the value
of deals, stage relationship, pipeline stage and list
membership.

- **Communications** – The tracking of email inbox
messages, calls, chat bot, live chat and text, SMS and
social media messages is key in the modern business
world, and a good CRM will make all of this easy
and keep it centrally available. The best systems will
increase efficiency by allowing you to set up response
email templates and snippets of text that can be used
for scaling your comms.

- **Admin and management** – The ability to connect up
your business and individual emails from Microsoft
365 or Google Workspace, link calendars for meeting
management, set up tasks, store documents, send quotes
and handle support tickets is all built in to modern CRM
systems to increase efficiency and save time.

If there is one thing you take from this chapter, make sure
it is a commitment to get a modern CRM system at the heart
of your business – it will be a game changer for you.

Build and develop a modern growth-driven website

Your website is such a critical part of your system; in fact, I
would say it is your biggest lead generation and marketing asset.

Your website is your best salesperson. When set up
correctly, it will move people along their buying journey,
answer their questions and develop a natural sales conversation. Before potential customers reach out to you as a

business, they can be pre-sold and 70% of the way towards making a buying decision.

Yet with all this said, it amazes me how many businesses still treat their website as little more than an online brochure. The website will usually consist of an about us page, a services page, a pricing page and a contact us page. If you are lucky, there may be a news blog buried in there somewhere with three posts per year. The majority are outdated and not fit for purpose, mainly due to the fact that the way businesses approach the process is to spend a large amount of money developing the website, then tick that off as done.

I will put this bluntly: every day, prospective customers are researching and looking for solutions to their problems and challenges. They are searching for answers to questions, and if they come across your website and it is one of the above 'brochure' sites, then you will miss out on the opportunity to get a conversation started with these people, as they will leave and go somewhere else.

In short, you must turn your website into a useful community hub for your visitors, full of valuable insights and information.

User experience is everything

Make sure it is fast, easy to navigate and mobile optimised. If your website takes longer than a few seconds to load, you will lose visitors and also get penalised by Google for slow loading pages, which will harm your SEO efforts.

Be human, holistic and helpful with your content

Just because your website is a digital platform does not excuse you from being human and personalising the experience visitors have on your site. Make sure you offer solution-based content that answers people's questions, videos that address their challenges, blog posts that educate and resources that help your clients start the process, such as guides and check-lists. You want your website visitors to consume, use and share your content. Focus on giving visitors multiple ways to do this.

Messaging and positioning

Position your business and solution correctly in the eyes of your website visitors. The rule of thumb I use is would a visitor arrive at your site and know immediately who you help, how you help them and why you do it better than anyone else?

Conversion focused

The best practice dictates that you should aim to convert 2%–5% of your website visitors into leads in your CRM. I can tell you that, in the majority of B2B businesses, they are lucky to convert 0.1% of their traffic, as they are not set up to do this.

Go be remarkable: The correct approach is to treat your website like any other digital asset, something that is constantly changing and evolving based on feedback from its users. I recommend looking at websites such as Gong[17] and Convert Kit[18] to see how a modern website looks, feels and behaves. See how they use chat bots, resources, messaging and a clean and simple design to

---

[17] www.gong.io/
[18] https://convertkit.com/

connect and engage the visitor. Research others in your sector who have already got it right and model yours on them. Above all, focus on being buyer-centric and not seller-centric.

Remarkable businesses embrace a growth-driven mindset of constantly improving the user experience and useful content and focusing on the highest value pages on the website. Each quarter, a new area of the site will be the focus for development, based on user feedback and data on what is working. My advice here is to embrace this approach yourself. Identify what is important first and build on this with quarterly reviews.

Save time and increase efficiency through administrative tools and software

As you build up your system, make sure it is increasing your efficiency, making the day-to-day life of your team easier and saving you all time.

The tools I recommend you look at here are:

- **Core business software** – for email, calendars, word processing, spreadsheets, presentations and cloud storage. The two leaders here are Google Workspace and Microsoft 365. I have used both, and while I have a slight preference for the Google suite, both offer all the functionality you need for a reasonable price, plus they will integrate with your CRM software in a couple of clicks.

- **Meetings planner** – Linked to your calendars, this tool should allow for the easy management and setting up of meetings. Use Calendly or HubSpot's built-in tool.
- **Tasks, project management and collaboration** – Use Trello, Asana or a tool such as Monday.com to allow you to manage tasks, projects and team collaboration.

Do not add any tool unless it is going to save time and increase productivity and efficiency. Your goal is to make people's lives easier and reduce friction wherever possible.

Marketing tools and software

The drivers of automation and digital transformation in most companies are usually the marketing or the sales team.

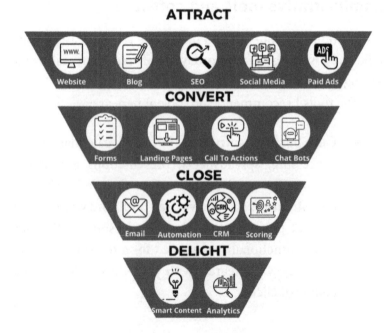

Lead generation is a key part of your processes, and building out a machine that can predictably attract new leads into the top of your funnel is critical when growing a remarkable seven-figure business. An example of how these tools may look in a modern marketing funnel is on page 160. The marketing tools that will drive effective lead generation are:

Modern content management system

Your CMS will be used for building your website on. The most popular are WordPress, Drupal, Joomla or my own CMS of choice – HubSpot.

Blogging

I would include this as part of your website, but it is so important to have a modern-looking blog that is easy to use. Create engaging blog posts with embedded videos, images and graphics that are fully search engine optimised to rank in the search engines for your target keyword phrases and the questions your audience is asking.

Paid ad management

A tool to manage your paid ad campaigns on Google Ads, LinkedIn ads and re-marketing campaigns is important so that you can quickly see where your positive ROI is being achieved and where the majority of leads are being generated from.

Search engine optimisation

This is important for an organic growth of traffic to your website, monitoring keywords and finding new opportunities. I use a combination of Ahrefs, SEM Rush and HubSpot's built-in tools.

Social media tools

Use software such as Hootsuite, Sprout Social or Meet Edgar for scheduled posting on Twitter, LinkedIn, Facebook and Instagram, monitoring conversations and handling inbound messages. Social media metrics and reporting must be built in here to measure effectiveness.

Conversion tools

All the traffic you control must go to dedicated landing pages and not your homepage, so you need tools that allow for the creation of landing pages, forms, calls to action and thank you pages and the easy creation of campaign assets and conversion reporting.

Email marketing and workflow automation

The ability to market effectively through email sequences and marketing emails to nurture and develop relationships is critical to your marketing effort. Using marketing automation is the key to doing this at scale.

Marketing dashboard and reporting

It is a good idea to set up live dashboards for campaigns and key marketing metrics because the ability to report back on what is working and what is not working and to quickly see what can be improved is crucial.

Do not try to do this manually, as it is not scalable. If you put these tools in place for your marketing team, you will be able to set up multiple successful marketing campaigns to ensure you attract a constant stream of warm leads into your pipeline for your sales team to pick up and convert into customers and revenue.

Give your sales team the tools to close deals and drive revenue

The critical process you develop alongside your lead generation is customer acquisition, how to engage and nurture leads and how to convert them into revenue and customers. Giving tools to your sales team or having the tools yourself to allow this to happen more efficiently and with more velocity will drive revenue growth and give you more confidence in your sales process.

The tools you need to focus on for your sales team are:

Customer relationship management (CRM)

As mentioned earlier in this chapter, this will allow your sales team to get a 360-degree view of all the conversations, engagement and activity that a lead has had with the business.

Lead scoring

This is the ability to identify best-fit leads that are highly engaged and clearly showing buying intent. A good CRM will allow you to score every action taken by a lead and use this to segment your top 20% most engaged leads at any one time. This is important to ensure that your sales efforts are focused on the right people, who are the most likely to convert, and not on people who are not engaged.

Email nurture

This involves sequences to nurture, share information and move a lead along the process. Tracking is key here to know when someone has opened and read an email or clicked on a link.

Email templates and snippets

Save time and increase efficiency with pre-prepared email templates and snippets of text for regularly asked questions.

Task automation

Increase efficiency with the automated setting of tasks and assigning of contacts and leads.

Video email tools

With more effective outreach using video tools such as Vidyard.com, you can send personalised videos embedded in emails, which will increase engagement and open rates.

Sales pipeline automation

This is the ability to run multiple pipelines for your business, with clearly defined stages that each lead moves along towards a sale.

Cloud-based document storage with tracking

The key here is that you or your sales team can easily access and send important documents across to a prospective client and see when they open and read it.

Meeting links

These allow for the easy organisation of meetings and presentations.

Video meeting tools

Use tools such as Zoom, Teams or Google Hangouts to enable video meetings alongside face-to-face meetings.

Playbooks

The processes for your sales approach should be laid out in playbooks, scripts and templates so that it happens the same way every time and is constantly evolving to be more effective. This also allows for the effective onboarding of new sales team members quickly and efficiently, increasing the success rate.

All these tools will help your sales team to sell more efficiently and at an increased velocity and allow for accurate reporting back on the effectiveness of your sales conversion and process.

Delighting your customers with remarkable delivery

I have mentioned a few times in this book the importance of delivering a remarkable product, service or solution to your customer and ensuring that this delivery is replicable and happens the same way every time, to the highest standard. Automating as much of your delivery process as possible is the secret to doing this at scale.

I will not be going deep into platforms in this section, as every industry and sector will have specific platforms unique to them, such as:

- Enterprise resource planning (ERP) software that oversees day-to-day business activities such as accounting, procurement, project management, risk management, compliance and supply chain operations
- Warehouse management software (WMS) for logistics and warehousing businesses
- Cybersecurity software in the cyber industry
- Product-led growth software in the SaaS industry

The list is as varied as the industries that use them. The rule here is to make sure you do your due diligence and are using a well-supported piece of cloud-based software that has the ability to integrate with other apps and software.

I say this because I come across so many pieces of outdated ERP software that are running on physical servers, have not been updated for ten years and do not talk to anything else, especially in the manufacturing and engineering sector. This is actually blocking growth rather than supporting it.

Constant improvement and evolution through service and support

Remarkable companies make it their mission to listen to their customers, with the aim of constantly improving and evolving their offering and user experience in every part of their business, so make sure you have the software and tools to enable you to do this predictably every time.

- Survey Monkey – To automate the sending and processing of feedback surveys
- Chat bots and live chat – For customers to get instant answers to questions
- Support ticketing – To deal with any support queries quickly and efficiently
- Email automation – Post-sale customer email sequences requesting feedback, reviews and testimonials
- Knowledgebase – Help customers to help themselves by building up a powerful knowledgebase: a library of articles and videos that cover the most frequently asked support questions. When done correctly, these articles can also rank in Google.

All these tools are designed to show that you appreciate your customers and are there to help them at every step of the journey.

Finance – Cloud-based accounting software

Finally, I will touch on the use of modern cloud-based accounting software. This will also integrate seamlessly with your business system, allowing financial data to sync backwards and forwards into your CRM.

The three main systems to look at are:

- Xero[19] – This is my personal choice and I have used it for the past eight years. It is incredibly powerful but also easy to use and keep up to date. It also integrates completely with HubSpot to allow invoicing and

---

[19] www.xero.com

financial data to be available in my dashboards and reporting.

- Sage[20] – This was the market leader in accounting software for years but seemed a little slow to embrace digital and cloud-based software. It has now caught up, however, and its offering of accounting, payroll and HR software is impressive.
- Quick Books[21] – This is another solid offering for small businesses and worth considering.

All three of these are affordably priced and offer powerful functionality to keep you on top of the numbers. They will help you save time managing expenses and revenue and tracking analytics to give you real-time information on the health of your business. Don't be one of the 50% of small businesses who are still not embracing cloud-based accounting.

Summary

Now is the time to get started on building your connected system of tools and software – a technology stack that will enable alignment, increase efficiency and drive growth at scale.

Make sure you focus on ensuring the eight key elements of your system work in harmony:

- CRM
- Website
- Administration and communication tools
- Marketing tools

---

[20] www.sage.com

[21] www.quickbooks.intuit.com

- Sales tools
- Operational delivery
- Service and support tools
- Finance tools

I recommend you take a good look at HubSpot.[22] It can do much of the heavy lifting for you and will integrate with other tools in your system to give you a true closed-loop system of data reporting that will allow you to make the right decisions to grow your business as you push towards seven figures and beyond.

Exercise #10 – Set up your CRM

I want you to go back over the research you did at the end of Chapter 4 and choose your CRM platform, get it set up, clean your existing customer and lead data and import that data into your new CRM system.

Don't move on to Chapter 11 until you have done this.

---

[22] www.hubspot.com

11. Metrics that matter

The power of digital is that you can measure everything

Over the past 30 years of owning and growing businesses, everything has changed. What used to take me weeks of data analysis to work out I can now see in a live dashboard or run a report on in a matter of seconds.

The fact is that digital allows you to measure everything, so you have no excuse for not knowing exactly what is working, what is not working and what can be improved to work better, in real time. As you build out your systems from the previous chapter, you will start to create more and more metrics and data points. In fact, the major problem I see with business owners is that they get overwhelmed with the amount of data being generated and with interpreting what it means.

The way to overcome this is to focus on a small number of metrics that matter; these are the outcome metrics that will have a direct impact on your growth goals.

I want you to step back from this and say to yourself: what data do I need to see to know if I am on or off track with my business growth?

Then, what are the key metrics to measure that will feed into these overall growth metrics?

When we talk about metrics that matter, these are the core metrics you need to track and run your reporting and dashboards around and they consist of three types – lead, lag and present. Let's look at each.

Lead metrics

These are the activities you are measuring that will directly impact the lag metric or outcome. So back to our example of improving our Net Promoter Score, you could invite customers to a live event – the more that attend these events, the more they will feel you appreciate them and the higher the NPS score you will receive. The number of event attendees is a lead metric that has a direct impact on your lag metric or NPS score. Your marketing and sales metrics are a mixture of activity and outcome metrics, so remember to measure them as such.

Lag metrics

These are the metrics for the outcome, so a good example here would be a goal to increase customer satisfaction in your business, and a good lag metric to measure would be your Net Promoter Score (NPS), which will either go up or down. The problem here is that these metrics are measured after an activity, so they are too late to change behaviour in the business. Your lag metrics will be your long-term goal metrics, so they are traffic, lead, customer acquisition and revenue generated. The ten metrics I asked you to identify in the exercise at the end of Chapter 2 are all your lag metrics.

Present metrics

These fall between lag and lead metrics. You will use present metrics to determine if something is working and improve on it. Again, back to our customer satisfaction example, you could measure how many of the event attendees gave an increased NPS score. This would let you know quickly if your event strategy was working, and if it was not giving the required outcome, you could start improving areas of your event until it was. Your sales team also has metrics that can be measured to ensure that their activity is having the required effect on new customer acquisition and revenue, so these can indicate where your sales process needs improving. A good example is if you look at your CRM. Is your sales team adding leads each day? If not, what training or approach do you need to adopt to ensure they are?

As I help clients understand these different types of metrics, I often see the clarity return to the way they view data and data analysis. So spend time looking at your own business and deciding what is important to know and what is just noise. In the following parts of this chapter I will move through your business funnel and identify some of the metrics you should measure in each of the five key areas of business growth.

Growth metrics and revenue goals

Whenever I work with a client, we will always define the specific financial goal we are aiming to achieve, look at where we are now and then reverse engineer the key lag metrics that will act as the key performance indicators (KPIs) as to whether we are on or off track.

These eight business growth goals are:

1. **Specific financial growth goal** – We want to get to £1m turnover in the next two years.
2. **Annual net new revenue goal** – We need to add £250k net new revenue per year.

3. **Current average order value** – What is the current average order value? I know you may have a number of products and different order sizes from different clients, but take your last 100 orders, total them up and divide them by a hundred, e.g., your AOV is £5000.

4. **New customers or sales required** – How many net new customers are required in the next 12 months? Our current average order value is £5000, so to hit our goal of £250k additional revenue we need to generate 50 net new customers or customer orders. You now have a specific goal for your sales team.

5. **Sales cycle** – How long is your current sales cycle? As you map out your strategy for growth and forecast revenue, you must allow for this in your metrics. If it takes three months to land a new customer from initially speaking with them, then this must be allowed for in your lead time and forecasting.

6. **Conversion rate** – Lead to customer. I talk about this in more detail in the sales metrics, but this is an important figure. If your sales conversion rate is 20%, then you need to generate five leads for every one customer.

7. **Annual leads required** – To generate 50 new customers, we would need to have marketing generate 250 new leads or about 20 per month. Again, you now have a specific goal for your marketing team or marketing effort.

8. **Website conversion rate** – Use Google Analytics to identify what traffic your website is attracting on a monthly basis and then how many leads are currently generated from this traffic; we are looking for a conversion rate of 2%–5%. This will give you a goal

for how much traffic you need to generate through the website to hit the leads required. So to hit 20 leads per month you need to be seeing 1000 visitors a month to your website, then convert them at 2% to hit 20 leads.

As you can see, having a dashboard of these eight metrics and a monthly report generated will give you complete insight into whether you are on or off track with your overall growth goals, especially if you can feed financial data in from your accounting software so you have accurate revenue figures. Now you have these top-level goals and KPIs set up, it is time to go granular and look at the key metrics to measure that will feed into these overall goals.

Website traffic metrics

If you have taken action and developed a modern optimised website, you need to see how visitors are interacting with your website and make sure that your traffic generation is working if you are running social media campaigns, lead generation, SEO and organic traffic and paid campaigns.

The easiest way to do this is to set up a Google Analytics account through what Google is now calling their Marketing Platform.[23]

My word of warning here is to get this set up correctly, as when I work with clients, the number who think they have set it up correctly but haven't is a real concern.

The great thing about Google Analytics is that it measures everything and integrates into platforms such as HubSpot so

---

[23] https://marketingplatform.google.com

you can build out dashboards and reporting that is constantly correct and up to date.

Some of the metrics I would recommend you measure for website analytics include:

- **Visitors per day with a breakdown of new and returning visitors** – Important to understand if you are attracting fresh new traffic to your site or existing contacts are returning.
- **Session totals per day with a breakdown of new and returning visitors** – A session is not the same as a visitor, as a visitor could have two or three sessions.
- **Bounce rate percentage** – This will tell you how well people are engaging with your website pages. It measures how many people visit a page without taking any action and then leave.
- **Page views per session** – This measures how many pages a visitor views on average when they come to your site. An engaging website will have four to five pages visited per session.
- **Website visits by sources by day** – This is invaluable as it will show you what sources are working and driving traffic, so I would break down at least six sources of traffic: organic search, direct traffic, organic social, paid search, paid social and referrals.
- **Website visitors by device** – Desktop vs mobile devices. This will vary by industry, but you will see more and more of your visitors using mobile devices to access your website, so optimise for mobile traffic.
- **Top 10 pages** – Under behaviour in Google Analytics, you can get a list of which pages people are visiting the most on your website. You will nearly

always see the homepage in the #1 spot, followed by other pages. Again, when working with clients, I am aiming for at least five blog posts to appear in the top ten pages.

I use HubSpot for my main reporting dashboard and to run reports such as a traffic source report, which is invaluable for my clients, as they can see exactly what is working for driving traffic and converting into leads, and we have now added revenue into this too.

As you can see, understanding your website traffic and visitor behaviour does not need to be overwhelming if you get the right metrics in place. So now let's move on to turning that traffic into leads.

Marketing metrics

Marketing is all about lead generation, so your focus must be on how effective your lead generation efforts are.

The marketing metrics I would focus on are:

- **Leads generated per day and month** – You can have Marketing Qualified Leads (MQLs), but this is not the core metric here. I measure how many new leads or contacts are being added to the CRM each day and month.
- **Campaign metrics** – Which campaigns are running and where the leads are coming from. These would include social media campaigns, paid campaigns, product/service campaigns and seasonal campaigns. You may run Q1 or Q2 campaigns – make sure you can differentiate.

- **Email metrics** – How many sent, how many opened, how many link clicks and the click through rate.
- **Blog post views** – What your most popular blog posts are by number of views.
- **Landing page views** – Which of your landing pages are the most popular by views and submission rate percentage, i.e., people who actually take an action or complete a form.
- **Social media engagement** – Do not fall into the trap of measuring size of audience, likes or views. These are vanity metrics that have no direct impact on your lead generation. I would focus on engagement metrics, comments, shares, direct messages and link clicks to show you have functioning social media channels. Also, your traffic source report will show you how much traffic social is generating, then by clicking on this you can drill down to each platform. I know that LinkedIn drives more traffic to my website than Twitter or YouTube at present, but YouTube is catching up as I add more video content.
- **Paid ad campaign performance** – If you are running Google Ads and/or LinkedIn paid and re-marketing campaigns then you need to measure the ROI of the leads generated and the revenue that those leads are generating. If you can see that for every £1 you spend you are generating £2 to £3, then this is a great place to be.
- **Cost of customer acquisition** – A key figure for marketing is to measure the cost of each new customer as an average. This can then give you an accurate idea of what you need to invest in marketing to hit your

revenue goals. You need to keep driving this cost down by optimising and improving what you do.

These marketing metrics will give you a good idea of how your lead generation efforts are performing and where you need to improve.

Sales metrics

Great sales is all about activity, so measuring activity metrics and setting revenue goals is key to having a motivated sales team.

- **Revenue generated** – Your lag metric.
- **Leads generated** – These can be Sales Qualified Leads following a handover of MQLs from the marketing team.
- **Appointments** – Meetings and appointments scheduled with these leads to turn them into opportunities.
- **Presentations** – A solutions presentation following one or a number of meetings. A solutions presentation should be followed with a proposal or a straight 'yes' or 'no'.
- **Closed/Won** – Sales made following the presentation.
- **Closed/Lost** – Sales lost after the presentation. It is vital to record all of these to analyse ways to improve the sales process and to nurture and follow up on a monthly basis.
- **Number of calls** – Tracking the activity of phone and virtual calls made. I would define a call as an initial connect call, so a short 15-minute initial introduction call.

- **Number of emails sent** – The volume of emails sent on a weekly basis is a strong indicator of success.
- **Conversion rate percentage** – An accurate figure to measure the conversion of lead to customer. The average B2B business has a 1 in 5 or 20% conversion rate, so to improve this to 1 in 4 or 25% would drive a major uptick in revenue.
- **Sales pipeline conversion percentage** – Tracking the conversion rate percentage at each stage of your pipeline allows a constant improvement of your sales process, removing friction and increasing effectiveness.
- **Average order value** – This is a key metric for sales and also your revenue goal achievement, as this value needs to be moving up and increasing. This will directly affect how many net new customers per year you need to generate.
- **Sales cycle length** – It is vital to understand how long your sales cycle is and accurately be able to predict how long it will take from first conversations with a prospective customer to them signing an agreement and revenue to hit the bank. In most B2B businesses with a considered purchase, this can range from six months to two years, so it is important to take this into account in your forecasting and focus your sales team on reducing this time wherever possible.

'Fix your leaky bucket' is a term that I use a lot when discussing marketing and sales with clients. It is particularly true with conversion and sales metrics. There is little point in pouring more leads into a low-converting sales process and funnel, but once you have optimised this at each stage, you can then focus on adding volume, safe in the knowledge that the increased number of leads will convert.

Service metrics

We have discussed the importance of delighting our customers and supporting them post-sale. So what are the six key service metrics to measure?

- **Customer Satisfaction Score (CSAT)** – How happy are your customers with your product, service or solution? These are simple survey questions and the responses can be measured.
- **Net Promoter Score (NPS)** – I have discussed a number of times the importance of NPS, as it is a measure of customer loyalty and how likely they are to recommend your company.
- **Customer Retention Rate (CRR)** – This is the percentage of customers your business has retained over a given period. This is critical, as we know that 80% of our profits will come from 20% of our customers.
- **Customer Churn Rate (CCR)** – The opposite of CRR, this is measuring how many customers you have lost over a given period. You must be pro-active with both areas of retention and churn.
- **Total Number of Support Tickets** – This is a simple metric to track and will help you understand how you are performing but also how under pressure your service team are.
- **Customer Lifetime Value (CLV)** – A key metric to understanding your overall growth is how valuable a customer is to your business, not just purchase by

purchase but across the lifetime of the relationship they have with you. So how much do they spend and how long on average do they stay with you? You can see how this metric can affect how much you can afford to invest in acquiring new customers, so it can be another factor that helps you decide on marketing budgets for lead generation and sales budgets for customer acquisition.

There are many service and support metrics to measure, such as the number of reviews customers leave you, the number of referrals they give you and the testimonials they leave you, but the six above will help you understand how well you are doing initially.

> **Go be remarkable:** Build a growth dashboard for your business of the top 10–12 metrics so that, no matter where you are in the world, you can see how well your business is performing, and if things slow down, you will know exactly what to focus on to accelerate your growth again.

Summary

Every remarkable business will measure metrics that matter. The data never lies and the decisions you make when using data to replace opinion will always be stronger. You have the top-level decisions about whether your overall growth strategy is working, then you have granular metrics to help you make decisions on your lead generation, your marketing campaigns, your paid ads, the effectiveness of your sales process and how well you are delivering for your customers.

Metrics are so critical because the market is the ultimate decision-maker on whether you succeed or fail. The market will never lie to you; it will tell you whether it likes and understands what you do or not, and the data you have in front of you in black and white is always going to outperform your opinion.

Exercise #11 – Set up five growth dashboards and reports

I want you to go back to your CRM from the last chapter and set up five dashboards and reports for yourself. These will be:

1. **Business Growth Dashboard** – A top-level view of the eight most important metrics that will show you if you are on track or off track to hit your growth goal each year.
2. **Website Traffic Analytics** – A dashboard of eight to ten traffic metrics, including your overall website traffic on a monthly basis, what pages are the most popular, what blog posts people are reading and how visitors are engaging with your website.
3. **Marketing Metrics** – To show how effective you are being with the conversion of content, social media and traffic into leads. Make sure you build campaign metrics and lead source metrics into this, so you can see ROI in your lead generation easily.
4. **Sales Metrics** – At the very least, you need to set your LAPS report up into a dashboard so you are measuring Leads, Appointments, Presentations and

Sales generated. I would also add in activity metrics such as number of calls made, number of emails sent, etc. and sales pipeline metrics for measuring how leads are moving through the pipeline and where the blocks are that you need to improve.

5. **Service Metrics** – Finally, build out a dashboard measuring your key service and support metrics that will show you are delivering for clients.

12. Your remarkable seven-figure roadmap and tips for success

Anyone can build a remarkable seven-figure business

If there is one thing that I want you to take away from this book, it is the fact that, with a proven strategy, processes and systems in place, any B2B business owner can build a remarkable business that can propel them to seven figures and beyond.

If you align the way you market and sell with how your buyer now researches and understands their problems before assessing their options and making a buying decision, you will win every time. Do not fall into the trap of doing what you have always done because I can guarantee that this is not working – the world has changed around you and left you behind.

My advice is to change your mindset first. It is no coincidence that many of the exercises I set for you at the end of each chapter were to 'audit' where you are now and then plan out where you need to be and what needs changing.

So let's finish by getting you started and taking action.

Your roadmap to £1m turnover and beyond

I will start by simplifying what I have spoken about in this book and get you a roadmap set out of actions to take to get your business to £1m. If you are already at £1m, then use this same approach to drive more predictable growth and add another million onto your bottom line.

You want to create a business that you love as much as when you started it. Remember the excitement you had in those first few months, when you were full of energy and anything was possible. You want to have a business that gives you time rather than taking it away, a business that has consistently growing income streams so you never have to worry about money, a talented team around you that is running and improving on everything you do as a business, a business that gives you complete clarity on the future and a business that can be as big or small as you want.

So work through this checklist to give you the roadmap to that business:

1. **Audit** – Where are you now. Use my self-diagnostic scorecard[24] to help you get an overview of where you are strong and where you need to improve.
2. **Goals** – Write down your specific revenue goals and don't be vague. Paint a picture in your mind of what you want the business to look like, how many people, what your offices will look like, how many clients, etc.
3. **Gaps analysis** – What gaps do you have in knowledge, skills or resources that you need to fill?
4. **Opportunities** – Where are your quick wins and opportunities for growth?
5. **Challenges** – Where are your main blockers or challenges to growth?
6. **Timescales** – Set yourself specific timescales and milestones.

---

[24] https://bit.ly/SevenFigureBusinessScore

7. **Start with a strategy** – Go back through the chapters in this book and start by spending the next 8–12 weeks mapping out a detailed strategy for growth. Go deep into each of the 12 parts of your strategy.

8. **Plan a Strategy Launch Day** – Once you have completed your strategy, invite everyone in the business to a Strategy Launch Day event to align the entire business around the strategy and goals, plus the part each person will play in achieving those goals.

9. **Annual strategy review and revise session** – Your strategy is an evolving document, so make sure you spend a weekend at the start of each year reviewing and amending it to keep you on track.

10. **Culture** – Build a culture in the business. Use your origin story, your mission and your vision of the future to inspire and attract people to what you do.

11. **Find your purpose** – People are attracted to a purpose, especially when that purpose involves sustainability and the environment, so attach yourself to a purpose and turn your business into a force for good. A great starting point here is to start by looking at the United Nations Global Goals[25] and find one for the heart and one for the head. Then find a local charity to support that aligns with this purpose.

12. **Complete your sales plan** – Download the sales plan document[26] and work through the four pages to give you clear goals across the next 12 months. By the time

---

[25] www.globalgoals.org/

[26] https://goberemarkable.com/resources

you have finished your sales plan, you should have a clear idea of what actions you need to take.

13. **Complete your marketing plan** – The sales plan should allow you to plan out your marketing campaigns and have solid leads that need generating from these campaigns, so map out each in detail and what marketing assets need to be created for each. Make your marketing remarkable, not average.

14. **Process all the tasks you should not be doing** – You need your time to be focused on the high-value strategic work, so make sure you are disciplined and identify every task you should not be doing and delegate it to someone in your team. Complete 'how to' videos and document how you do it, step by step.

15. **Employ a virtual assistant** – Keep yourself organised by bringing in a virtual assistant to look after your diary, plan meetings and generally keep you on track. Do not try to find the cheapest – there are some amazing VAs out there, so find the best you can. Freeing you first is the goal.

16. **Employ a sales person** – The first person you employ has got to be in sales, someone to focus solely on business development and turning leads into customers and revenue. I know this is the biggest change for most businesses I work with, but people put it off for too long. Get someone good and then train them. You really want this person to have the capability to become your sales manager in the future, so, again, trying to save money here is false economy.

17. **Hire a marketer** – I say hire because this can be either a marketing agency or an in-house person, but, whichever way you go, you need to give them clear

goals on how many leads you expect to be generated each month and run through the marketing plan with them.

18. **Give your team the tools to succeed** – Set up your system and give your team the software, apps and tools it needs to succeed and you need to be able to measure performance and progress.

19. **Focus on remarkable delivery** – Your core product, service or solution must be developed, innovated and refined constantly. When this offering is truly remarkable, the majority of your problems will disappear.

20. **Measure everything** – Finally, make sure you have metrics, data and analysis on everything you are doing. I have said this multiple times in this book, but it will be this that makes the biggest difference in success or failure.

I want you to take these 20 points and use them to build your own roadmap to seven figures and beyond. I have seen time and time again how these elements work together to drive predictable and unstoppable growth for businesses, so use them and get started today.

My top five tips for remarkable success

1. **Go be remarkable** – Make it your core mission to make every touchpoint in your business remarkable so that however people come into contact with your business, they leave thinking: 'Wow, that was an amazing experience.' People will connect with you and your business on an emotional level first and then justify this with logic. People do business with people.

By making the experience personal and remarkable, you will do this every time. It is no coincidence that my website is called www.GoBeRemarkable.com.

2. **Be a specialist, not a generalist** – The single thing that has made the biggest difference to the businesses I have worked with is moving from a broad, wide focus to a deep, narrow focus and dominating that niche. We do this by identifying what the businesses do well, who they do it for, why they are passionate about doing it for that person and why they do it better than anyone else. My view is that any business can get to £1m turnover by focusing on solving one problem for one person better than anyone else. When you are a generalist it will nearly always come down to price, but when you are a specialist, people will want to work with you and price will be secondary, and in many cases irrelevant. Remember: this does not mean you can't have additional products, services and solutions in the future, but our goal is to get you to £1m first and then expand your offering. Specialists naturally have fewer competitors than generalists.

3. **Understand your buyer** – This is closely aligned to the previous tip. Once you know who you are targeting, make it your business to understand them better than they understand themselves. Make a list of their 50 pains, the source of those pains, the symptoms they experience, the cost to them and the consequence of not solving them. Then think about the mistakes they are making on a daily basis, the things they are doing and the things they are thinking that are

wrong and stopping them resolving their pains and challenges. Now make a list of the prizes or payoffs that they are looking to achieve by solving their problems, thinking and doing the right things. Make this an iterative process, where you are constantly adding to your understanding of these areas.

4. **Build your A-team** – I want you to focus on attracting talent to your business. Build a culture, mission and vision that will attract these people and make them want to work for you. You are building a team of 8–12 people and you need each one to be an A-player. As brutal as it sounds, do not settle for anything less, as you will find yourself hand-holding and never trusting them, which will hold you back and cause unrest amongst the rest of your team, who are giving their all.

5. **Plan, execute, measure and optimise** – Everything in your business from now on is being optimised to be remarkable. Do not be scared to test a theory by getting it in front of people, measuring the results, making improvements and returning to the market again. When you get this outcome-focused approach into every area of your business, you will build a strong 'can do' culture that is constantly searching for a better way to do something. This will accelerate your growth to greatness and to being remarkable faster than anything else. It also removes the fear of failure from your team, as they will realise that everything is a learning experience and a poor result is one step closer to a positive outcome.

The secret weapons of depth, focus and accountability

I nearly put this section into my five tips, but it is so fundamental to the success of so many businesses I have worked with over the years that I felt it deserved a section all to itself. I also hear these three elements from clients when I ask them what the biggest benefit of working with me on their business growth was.

- **Depth** – The ability to do deep work is critical to success in business, as so many owners are so wrapped up in their world and busy working in their business that they never stop to go deep and do the high-value strategic work needed to make the difference. They do a bit of shallow thinking and then go back to the low-value work in their business. In the modern world our ability to concentrate, learn and be productive will allow us to master hard things quickly and be remarkable in what we do.
- **Focus** – This is connected to depth and it is our ability to stay focused on the important things and not get interrupted or distracted. I love the analogy of focus being Follow One Course Until Successful, and this is encompassed in Tip #5 above on planning, executing, measuring and optimising. So many business owners I meet struggle to have clarity on what they need to be focusing on and why. As I have discussed, this always leads back to a lack of a strategy being in place.
- **Accountability** – As owners of businesses we are at the top, the boss, the one in charge of everything. But the biggest drawback to this structure is the lack of

accountability. Who are you accountable to? Who does your quarterly appraisal to tell you if you are doing a good job or not? Who is measuring your performance as a leader and owner? I love to challenge owners on this but in a healthy way, something that will bring the best out in them and also unlock some of the things that are holding them back. As we discussed in the previous chapter, the market is holding you accountable for your actions every day and, by setting up metrics and dashboards, you are then accountable for the results.

Go be remarkable: Build a circle of trusted advisors and bring in expertise where needed. On that last point, being the owner can be a lonely business and, alongside accountability, you need people you respect and trust in place to keep you on track and give you advice when things are tough – and they will be at times. I recommend building a 'board' of diverse skill sets who can support you as you grow. I act as a non-executive director on a few boards and the mix of people is always key, plus the ability to be open and discuss issues freely. The accountability a board gives you is a positive, and they should also support you in identifying the right things to focus on.

If you ever want any help and support to bring these into your business and feel that I can help you, then please feel free to reach out and discuss this with me. You can email me on richard@goberemarkable.com.

Summary

I hope this book has inspired you and, above all else, given you a formula to follow to take your business to seven figures. I know it will be hard work, but the rewards are worth it – getting to that lifestyle business where you start enjoying your work again, it gives you a good income and you get the time to spend on the things that really matter in your life, alongside your business.

Above all, the biggest reward I see for business owners who break through to this level is the ability to use their success for the greater good and leave a legacy that they made a difference. I personally used my business to give young people a start in their working lives and set up apprenticeships and took on graduates on internships, giving them a culture that they loved to work in but that also helped them thrive, build confidence and experience. I found this truly rewarding, especially when people I had mentored went on to greater things such as Rachel, who set up her own HubSpot Agency, or Isaac, who I mentored and who went on to work at Twitter.

These are the real rewards you will start to see in your own life, as well as the pride of running a successful business. So go get started today, and if you need any help, then make sure to reach out to me on richard@goberemarkable.com or visit the website www.goberemarkable.com – I look forward to hearing of your success.

Final Exercise #12 – Start your £1m roadmap today

I am going to leave you with one final exercise to make sure you take action today and don't just put this book down on a shelf and never act on what you have just read.

I want you to spend the next 20 days mapping out your £1m roadmap. So take one of the points each day and block out two hours to work deeply on that point. Then, at the end of the two hours, look at the point you are going to work on the next day and let your mind mull it over through the next 24 hours, then repeat.

Just start writing or typing everything that you have in your head and get it down on paper for each of the points. At this stage it is not about coming up with a polished plan; it is about making a list of high-priority tasks that you need to focus your time on.

The strategy phase of STEPS will start the process of polishing these ideas and crafting them into an effective strategy.

I repeat: block out two hours (I recommend first thing in the morning) to get writing. Commit to this time each day for the next 20 days and let me know how you are doing.

Conclusion:
There has never been
a better time to build a
£1m business

After 30 years of owning and building my own businesses and helping other people to build theirs, one thing is clear: we are living through the best time in history to be an entrepreneur and business owner.

Everything is in your favour when you approach it correctly. The modern connected world makes it possible for any B2B business of any size to compete and dominate a niche in a market. As a small and agile business, you can beat the big corporates, who are slow to respond and use their financial superiority to overwhelm you. You can disrupt a market to connect and engage with your target audience like never before, but also to understand that audience, what challenges they have, what mistakes they are making and what prizes they are seeking.

It is this – their ability to personalise the experience and remove friction for their buyers – that I see as the key for small businesses to thrive in the modern economy, making it easy to reach a buying decision and build the kind of loyalty that the big corporates can only dream of.

The future is yours, my friend, a future where you own the seven-figure business you deserve; one that gives you more fun, freedom and fulfilment while allowing you to create a legacy for the future. The only question is: are you ready to go out there and grab it?

I wish you well and can't wait to hear of your success. Go be remarkable.

References

Christensen, C., 'Foreword to the First Edition', in McChesney, C., Covey, S., Huling, J., Walker, B., and Thele, S., *The 4 Disciplines of Execution: Achieving Your Wildly Important Goals* (London: Simon & Schuster, 2021).

Godin, S., *Purple Cow: Transform Your Business by Being Remarkable* (United States: Penguin, 2005).

Priestley, D., *24 Assets* (United Kingdom: Rethink Press, 2017).

Sheridan, M., *They Ask, You Answer* (United States: John Wiley & Sons, 2017).

Tyre, D., and Hockenberry, T., *Inbound Organization* (United States: John Wiley & Sons, 2018).

Further resources

'Leaders are readers' and to build a remarkable business you really need to read the right books that will not just give you the 'what' but also the 'how'. Here are the books I would recommend and also the blogs and websites that I trust and use on a daily basis. I hope these help.

Top ten must-read books

Newport, C., *Deep Work: Rules for Focused Success in a Distracted World* (London: Piatkus, 2016) – Learn how to master difficult things quickly and produce at an elite level in speed and quality.

McChesney, C., Covey, S., Huling, J., Walker, B., and Thele, S., *The 4 Disciplines of Execution: Achieving Your Wildly Important Goals* (United Kingdom: Simon & Schuster, 2021) – A simple, repeatable and proven formula for executing your most important strategic priorities.

Collins, J., *Good to Great* (United States: Random House Business, 2001) – The seminal book on building a great business, uncovering the underlying variables that enable any organisation to make the leap from good to great.

Tyre, D., and Hockenberry, T., *Inbound Organization: How to Build and Strengthen Your Company's Future Using Inbound Principles* (United States: John Wiley & Sons, 2018) – The go-to authority on growing better by using inbound principles.

Priestley, D., *24 Assets* (United Kingdom: Rethink Press, 2017) – Uncover how to create a digital, scalable, valuable and fun business that will thrive in a fast-changing world.

Godin, S., *Purple Cow: Transform Your Business by Being Remarkable* (United States: Penguin, 2005) – A short read but full of advice on how to transform your business by being remarkable.

Brunson, R., *Traffic Secrets: The Underground Playbook for Filling Your Websites and Funnels with Your Dream Customers* (United States: Hay House, 2020) – Learn how to identify and find your people so you can focus on changing their world with the products and services you sell.

Sheridan, M., *They Ask, You Answer* (United States: John Wiley & Sons, 2017) – The bible when it comes to content marketing and inbound sales, Marcus shares an approach that works for any business in any sector.

Shanks, J., *Social Selling Mastery: Scaling Up Your Sales and Marketing Machine for the Digital Buyer* (United States: John Wiley & Sons, 2016) – The best book I have ever read on social selling and how to use LinkedIn to generate a constant stream of leads for a B2B business.

Pink, D.H., *To Sell Is Human: The Surprising Truth About Persuading, Convincing and Influencing Others* (United Kingdom: Canongate Books, 2013) – The go-to guide for modern selling and how to be human, holistic and helpful in your customer acquisition.

Three blogs to bookmark

HubSpot (https://blog.hubspot.com/) – If you're a business that wants to grow better, then this is the blog for you.

Digital Marketer (www.digitalmarketer.com/blog/) – Ryan Deiss' digital marketing blog is an incredible resource and one I read daily.

Neil Patel (https://neilpatel.com/blog/) – This used to be all SEO based, but the depth of content over the past few years has diversified across digital business growth and metrics. Read, learn and put into action.

Acknowledgements

Alison Jones, Practical Inspiration Publishing (www.practicalinspiration.com) – For making this book a reality and working so hard to make it the best it can be.

Daniel Priestley – For making me take the action to write this book when part of his Key Person of Influence Accelerator Programme with Dent Global (www.dent.global).

Dan Tyre, Sales Director at HubSpot and Inbound Fellow (www.dantyre.com) – For his friendship, his mentoring and agreeing to write such a wonderful foreword.

Laura Nickson from Laura Next Door (www.lauranextdoor.com) – For her illustrations used in the book.

Alen Zenjko from Few Dots Design in Zagreb (www.linkedin.com/in/alenzanjko/) – For his graphics, illustrations and designs.

Sebastian Bates, Founder of Non Profit 'Bates Foundation' and CEO of The Warrior Academy LLC (www.sebastianbates.com) – For his mentorship and support over the Key Person of Influence Accelerator.

And, of course, my six incredible beta readers:

Richard Warrilow, owner of Declaration Ltd, world leaders in technical marketing support (www.declaration.co.uk).

Austen Hempstead, owner of Selling is a Skill and one of Europe's leading sales coaches and trainers (www.austen-hempstead.com).

Gary Davies, owner of Gary Davies Photography and one of the UK's leading commercial photographers (www.garydavies.photography).

David Allen, owner of Allen Signs (www.allen-signs.co.uk) and Vice President of the International Sign Association UK (www.uksigns.org).

Tony Smith, Director of Genius Solutions (www.genius-technologysolutions.com) and Business Mentor at Oxford Brookes Business School.

Richard Bell, Director, Consultant and Trainer at NeuroEducation (www.linkedin.com/in/richard-bell-10193a138/).

The author

Richard Mawer is the Founder and CEO of Ignite Growth Consultancy, a B2B business growth consultancy. He works exclusively with B2B clients, using proven strategies, processes and systems to build a remarkable business that will scale to £1m turnover and beyond.

Over the past 30 years he has grown eight of his own businesses and helped hundreds of business owners to grow theirs, including one client who he worked with through to a £28m exit and another through to an £8m acquisition.

He is an expert in business strategy, processes and systems and, over the past decade, has created the STEPS Growth Method to give business owners a step-by-step approach to growing a 'remarkable' business that is resilient to fluctuations in the economy, attracts a constant stream of new clients and allows the owner to grow the remarkable business that they deserve, whether that be a £1m lifestyle business or an eight-figure performance business.

You can connect with Richard on:

Social media

LinkedIn – www.linkedin.com/in/richardmawer/
Twitter – https://twitter.com/RichardAMawer

Websites

www.ignitegrowth.co.uk
www.goberemarkable.com

Email

richard@ignitegrowth.co.uk
richard@goberemarkable.com

Index